Back to the Basics of Recovery

How to take the Twelve Steps "quickly and often"

For more information scan Blue QR Code

Back to the Basics of Recovery

How to take the Twelve Steps "quickly and often . . ."

using a modern, gender neutral version of the 1940's Beginners' Meeting format modified for "anyone and everyone interested in a spiritual way of life."

Wally P.

Faith With Works Publishing Company
Tucson, AZ

Published by Faith With Works Publishing Company
P.O. Box 91648, Tucson, AZ 85752-1648
tel: (520) 297-9348 / fax: (520) 297-7230 / e-mail: wallyp@theriver.com
http://www.aabacktobasics.org

First Edition, First Printing: February 2016
Second Printing, August 2016
Third Printing, April 2017

Library of Congress Cataloging -in-Publication Data

P., Wally, 1945-
Back to the basics of recovery: how to take the Twelve Steps "quickly and often."
p. cm.
Includes bibliographical references and appendices
LCCN: 2001-131462
ISBN 13: 978-0-9657720-1-3
ISBN 10: 0-9657720-1-2

1. Twelve Steps. 2. Addiction Recovery. 3. Alcoholism Recovery. 4. Compulsive Behavior Recovery. 5. Twelve Step Program for All Addictions. 6. Gender Neutral Big Book Passages. I. Title

Printed in the United States of America

Dedication

This book is dedicated to the thousands of people who have conducted Beginners' Meetings and helped make ***Back to Basics*** one of the most effective and successful methods for taking people through the Twelve Steps. It is also dedicated to the many hundreds of thousands who have had their lives changed as the direct result of taking the Steps based on a format from the mid-1940's.

Since its publication in 1997, ***Back to Basics*** has proven, beyond a shadow of doubt that, "It works–it really does." Over the years, members of other fellowships and programs have adapted ***Back to Basics*** for a number of addictions and compulsive disorders.

I commend those who have demonstrated the universality of the process developed by Dr. Bob and many of the pioneers during the early days of the recovery movement. This book is the author's attempt to update their original program so it can be used in treatment centers, after care facilities, half-way houses, recovery homes, correctional facilities, and other Twelve-Step fellowships. The format applies to all addictive and compulsive behaviors and the "Big Book" passages are gender neutral.

Contents

Acknowledgments

I will be forever grateful to the thousands of people who have assisted me on this journey. These include numerous Twelve Step host committees, treatment center alumni coordinators, halfway house and recovery home managers, prison and jail staff members, and mental health professionals. I am most appreciative of their enthusiastic support for this life-saving work. Now, that the format has been time-tested and proven and is making a significant difference within the recovery community, I owe a debt of gratitude to those who came before me and pioneered the process.

I want to thank those who provided feedback from their first hand experiences taking people through the Twelve Steps "quickly and often." You have exhibited a determination and dedication to "making a difference" that is most commendable. I know many of you have taken a "lot of heat" for your efforts, but you stood your ground and made it clear that "it's all about saving lives."

You have shown me numerous ways to make the process more efficient and effective. I have taken your suggestions to heart, beginning in 1992 when I began making archival presentations. After that first event, an old-timer come up and said, "Keep it up, kid. You've nailed it. This is the MTV generation. You've made the process multimedia and you're moving people through the work in thirty second sound bites."

I also wish to acknowledge James H., my spiritual guide from 1996-2006. His sobriety date was December 12, 1934. When James passed away, he was 100 years old and 71 years sober. In 2000, I wrote a tribute to him titled, ***How to Listen to God.*** This book explains how Bill W., Dr. Bob, James H., and the first one hundred took the Steps before the "Big Book" was written.

On numerous occasions, James explained to me that the program of recovery in the 1930's encompassed all addictive and compulsive behaviors. It was James who convinced me that the "Big Book" could easily be modified to take "anyone and everyone interested in a spiritual way of life" through the simple and straightforward recovery process. I thank you James for helping lead the way.

Back to the Basics of Recovery

How to take the Twelve Steps "quickly and often"

Introduction

On October 30, 1988, I became a member of the Twelve-step community. Shortly after walking into the rooms, a man who knew the "original" program of recovery guided me through all Twelve Steps in about four hours. He told me that in the early days people took the Steps "quickly and often." However, it didn't take me long to realize that by the late 1980's very few people were taking the Steps this way.

Shortly after receiving a one year medallion, my sponsor sat me down and said, "Wally, I'm not going to be alive much longer, but if you remember this one thing, you won't find it necessary to relapse, whether I am here or not. ***If you don't know where we came from, you'll never know what a miracle this program truly is.***" How prophetic those words turned out to be. My sponsor passed away six weeks later, and I have been studying the history of the Twelve-step movement ever since our one year anniversary meeting.

Within two weeks, I flew to Akron, OH to attend a speaker meeting held at the home of Dr. Bob and Anne Smith. There I listened to eight people, sponsored by Dr. Bob in the 1940's, who had also taken the Steps in a matter of hours. They talked about the simplicity of the recovery process and how they were still working this "original" program four to five decades later. That meeting became a turning point in my life. Right then and there, I made a commitment to pass on this "original" program as practiced by my sponsor, by Dr. Bob's sponsees, and, as I later learned, by many of the early members.

In 1992, I was elected Area Archivist, a keeper of the records, for the state of Arizona. One year into my two year term, I was approached by a number of "trusted servants" who asked me to write a book about the Intergroup and Central Offices in the 1940's. At the time very little was known about their contribution to the early success of the recovery movement.

This assignment gave me open access to numerous Intergroup and Central Office archives along with the Hazelden archives in Center City, MN and the GSO archives in New York City.

After two years of intensive research, I released the book on the history of the Intergroup and Central Offices. My examination of the records revealed that throughout North America, Beginner's Meetings were held on a regular basis. In these meetings, attendees took all Twelve Steps in four, one-hour sessions. This meeting format contributed significantly to the 50 to 75% recovery rate that was achieved during this period of time.

One of my archival mentors, who had been leading Beginners Meetings for more than forty years, told me the only way to understand the efficiency and effectiveness of these meetings was to conduct them myself. This I did. After numerous presentations over a two year period, along with interviews of hundreds of old-timers who were involved in the Beginners' Meetings of the 1940's and early 1950's, I wrote the book titled, ***Back to Basics***.

The return to this "original" meeting format was a major "game changer" for the recovery community. Meetings by the thousands sprang up throughout the United States, Canada, and around the world. Recovery rates soared. There were naysayers of course, but they were quickly swept aside by the flood of people who had "recovered from a seemingly hopeless state of mind and body" in these Beginners' Meetings.

Since 1997, I've been conducting one-day workshops using a modified version of the "original" Beginners' Meeting format. These events are usually held on a Saturday. We start at 9:30 in the morning and by 4:30 that afternoon everyone, including myself, has taken all Twelve Steps.

Over the years, I have personally guided more than 100,000 people through the process. Thousands of others have been leading meetings and at this time (2016), more than 700,000 have taken the Twelve Steps "quickly and often," with dramatic results.

I fully realize this is the "kindergarten" version of the Steps. I sincerely hope that every person who takes the Steps in the Beginners' Meetings will take them again and again in more depth and detail and study the "Big Book" over and over in the months and years ahead.

I have taken the Steps on numerous occasions using various "high school" and "college" formats. But, for whatever reason, God has chosen me and thousands of others to present the Steps in a simplified fashion.

A detractor once described ***Back to Basics*** as the "paint-by-numbers" version of recovery. I believe he was absolutely correct. ***Back to Basics*** is just the beginning of the recovery journey. But, according to the pioneers, we don't begin in high school or college, we begin in kindergarten.

One of the four Akron pamphlets written in the 1940's, at the request of Dr. Bob, is titled, ***A Guide to the Twelve Steps***. This pamphlet is still available today. It provides considerable insight into the early program as practiced by the early members:

> "It is important that the newcomer be introduced to the Twelve Steps at as early a date as possible. If you feel the Steps are a bit too complicated at first, you can introduce them to your (newcomer) in a simplified form, going into the complete program later."

About fifteen years ago I began making presentations at treatment centers, aftercare facilities, halfway houses, and correctional institutions. I realized many of the people in these "rooms" had problems other than alcohol, so I started modifying ***Back to Basics*** to be all-inclusive. After more than a decade of experience helping newcomers through the recovery process within the treatment community, I am now publishing the format I have used all these years at these locations.

The four chapters of this book are the Beginners' Meetings as presented today to "anyone and everyone interested in a spiritual way of life." The workshops I conduct using this format include PowerPoint slides, music, lunch, laughter, and a process that "works-it really does."

Sometime during the course of each event, I usually say, "I have the best seat in the house. I get to watch you recover right before my very eyes." It is a transformation I have witnessed more than 100,000 times.

A couple of years ago I wrote an article titled, "The Window of Opportunity." In it I made the following statement:

> On pages 13-14 of the "Big Book," we read that Bill W., while in detox at Towns Hospital in New York City, took the Steps in one day, recovered, and never drank again. In the chapter titled, "A Vision for You," we learn that Dr. Bob relapsed after a couple of weeks on the program because he had not made his Ninth Step amends. He made them in one day and never drank again.
>
> Later in this chapter, we learn that Bill D. (AA # 3) took the steps while he was being withdrawn from alcohol at Akron City Hospital. He too never drank again.
>
> In the story, "He Sold Himself Short," Dr. Bob took Earl T. through the Steps in "three or four hours." The pioneers repeated this process hundreds of thousands of times during the early days with remarkable success.
>
> I know there are those who are skeptical that the Steps are simple and can be taken "quickly and often." At one time, so was I. Then a friend pointed out to me that the only words used in the "Big Book" to describe Steps One through Nine are "next," "at once," "immediately," and "we waste no time."
>
> Recently, he told me the reason he takes newcomers through the Steps quickly is because of "the window of opportunity." This is how he explains the "window":
>
> > When a newcomer enters the Twelve-step community, whether from a treatment cen-

> ter, detox, or the street, he or she passes through a window of opportunity–a period of time when he or she is most "teachable." How long does a person remain in this state? In other words, how much time does it take a newcomer to realize the pain and suffering he or she is experiencing in recovery is greater than the pain and suffering he or she remembers when "out there" using? How much time do we have to alleviate this pain?
>
> Do we have a year? Absolutely not! Do we have a month? Sometimes we do, sometimes we don't. Do we have a week? For many, that may be pushing it. What if we only have today? What if we assume the newcomer is going to relapse tomorrow (and in many cases this is true). Why not take him or her through the Steps today in order to prevent that relapse tomorrow?

Back to the Basics of Recovery contains a message of hope for those who have been struggling with recovery either because the process has never been explained to them, or else it has been presented to them in a way that is so complicated they have given up on ever getting "clean and sober."

This book will change all that. **"There is a solution,"** and it is simple and straightforward. I thank the Twelve-step pioneers for revealing it to me so I could "pass it on" to you.

Chapter 1

Session #1–Overview and Steps 1, 2 and 3

WELCOME to the first of four ***Back to the Basics of Recovery*** meetings that will change your life! During these sessions, we will guide you through the Twelve Steps as described in the "Big Book,"and you will recover from **"a seemingly hopeless state of mind and body."**

We have found a way out–an answer to the insidious illnesses of addictive and compulsive behaviors. We are here to share our solution with you—a spiritually based **"program of action"** that will provide you with a new way of living beyond your wildest dreams.

Our names are ___________ and ___________, and we will be your guides for this meeting. During this session we will take the first three Steps.

The directions for taking the Steps are in the "Big Book" of ***Alcoholics Anonymous.*** Although this book deals primarily with alcoholism, it can be applied to any addictive or compulsive behavior.

The "Big Book" was first published in April 1939. It was written by several of the first 100 men to recover from alcoholism. Since then, people all over the world have used the "Big Book" as a textbook for recovery from any number of disorders. For these sessions, we have modified the applicable "Big Book" passages so they are gender neutral and applicable for all addictive and compulsive disorders.

So we can complete each session within an hour and still have time for questions, we request that you write down anything that you do not understand or need clarified and save it until the end of the session. We will answer questions at that time.

In order for the process to work, participants need to be matched up with those who are willing to help guide them through the Steps. This is a **WE** program. No one goes through the recovery process alone.

We attend the sessions together,
We read the "Big Book" together,
We take the Twelve Steps together, and
We recover together.

So that everyone can better understand what is expected of them , we are going to explain some of the guidelines for being a sharing partner:

For the Sharing Partner:

A. Your primary obligation is to attend all four sessions in order to take the Twelve Steps and offer encouragement and moral support to your partner. The conditions for being a sharing partner are:

   1. to be actively involved in your own Twelve-Step recovery,
   2. to be willing to listen to what your partner has to say, and
   3. to keep everything that is shared strictly

confidential.

B. We will guide you through the Twelve Steps by reading the appropriate parts of the "Big Book" to you. If you follow the directions provided by the "Big Book" authors, you too will experience the **"personality change sufficient to bring about recovery."**

C. The Fourth Step consists of a simple assets and liabilities checklist that you fill out during the second session. If you believe your partner satisfies the conditions of a **"closemouthed, understanding friend,"** please discuss your checklist with him or her. If your inventory contains specific items that you feel should be shared with a third party such as a person of the clergy, an attorney, a psychologist, or a counselor, explain this to your sharing partner. Make a commitment to your partner as to when, where, and with whom you will share those portions of your checklist.

D. Between the third and fourth sessions, share your Eleventh Step guidance with your partner so he or she can see how two-way prayer is working in your life.

Before we can begin, we need to make sure everyone has a sharing partner. First, we'd like the women to stand–all those who are here to take the Steps or help guide others through the Steps.

(Have the women stand.)

Now, if your sharing partner is with you right now in this room, we would like both of you to be seated.

(After the sharing partners have been seated,)

For those who are still standing, we would like for you to point to someone. After you're paired up with another person, we'd like both of you to sit down.

(If there is one woman left standing,)

Is there a woman here who is willing to work with two others? If so, please stand so this person can see who you are. Thank you. We will have the opportunity to meet with our sharing partners immediately after this meeting.

Now that all the women have sharing partners, let's do the same thing with the men. Will the men please stand–all those who are here to take the Steps or help guide others through the Steps.

(Have the men stand.)

Now, if your sharing partner is with you right now in this room, we would like both of you to be seated.

(After the sharing partners have been seated,)

For those who are still standing, we would like for you to point to someone. After you're paired up with another person, we'd like both of you to sit down.

(If there is one man left standing,)

Is there a man here who is willing to work with two others?

If so please stand so this person can see who you are. Thank you. Please be seated.

Now that everyone has a sharing partner, we can proceed. Let's start with the first paragraph in the Forward of the "Big Book," which is on Roman numeral page 13 (xiii). It states:

> WE . . . are more than one hundred men and women who have recovered from a seemingly hopeless state of mind and body. To show other(s) . . . *precisely how we have recovered* is the main purpose of this book. . . ."
>
> (pg. xiii, para. 1, lines 1-5, edited)

So, the "Big Book" authors immediately tell us that the purpose of this book is to show us how to recover from our addictive or compulsive behaviors. This is a revolutionary statement, because before the "Big Book" was written, there was very little hope for us. Now, anyone who is willing to follow the directions **THEY** have provided, can overcome their difficulties.

This message of hope is expressed again in the third paragraph on page 17:

> "The tremendous fact for every one of us is that we have discovered a common solution. We have a way out on which we can absolutely agree, and upon which we can join in . . . harmonious action. This is the great news this book carries to those who (want relief from their suffering)."
>
> (pg. 17, para. 3, lines 1-5, edited)

In the first paragraph on page 44, the authors tell us what it is going to take to recover. Starting with the fourth line, they write:

> ". . . If, when you honestly want to, you find you cannot quit entirely, or . . . you have little control over (your thoughts or actions), you . . . probably (have a problem). If that be the case, you may be suffering from an illness which only a spiritual experience will conquer."
>
> (pg. 44, para. 1, lines 4-9, edited)

To make sure everyone understands what we just read, we are going to read the last sentence again:

> **"If that be the case, you may be suffering from an illness which ONLY a spiritual experience will conquer."**

We now know what we have to do in order to recover. We must undergo a change in perception–a spiritual transformation.

Let's see what we can learn about this spiritual transformation. In the first paragraph on page 45, the "Big Book" authors state:

> "Lack of power, that was our dilemma. We had to find a power by which we could live, and it had to be a *Power greater than ourselves*. Obviously. But where and how were we to find this Power?
>
> "Well, that's exactly what this book is about. Its main object is to enable you to find a Power greater

than yourself which will solve your problem. . . ."

(pg. 45, para. 1, lines 1-4; para. 2, lines 1-3)

Back to the Basics of Recovery is not a religious program. We're free to call this Power by any name we wish, as long as it is a **"Power greater than ourselves."** The "Big Book" authors use many different names for this Power including **"Creative Intelligence," "Universal Mind," "Spirit of the Universe," "Creator,"** and **"Great Reality,"** among others. Sometimes they call this Power, **"God,"** but they use the word God merely for convenience rather than for any religious purpose. Please refer to this Power by any name you believe in or feel comfortable with.

So, in order to recover, we have to find a **"Power greater than ourselves."** But where are we going to find this Power? The authors answer this question in the second and third paragraphs on page 55:

> "Actually we were fooling ourselves, for deep down in every man, woman, and child, is the fundamental idea of God. It may be obscured by calamity, by pomp, by worship of other things, but in some form or other it is there. . . .
>
> " . . . Sometimes we had to search fearlessly, but (the Power) was there. (It) was as much a fact as we were. We found the (Power) deep down within us. In the last analysis it is only there that (the Power) may be found. . . ."
>
> (pg. 55, para. 2, lines 1-5; para. 3, lines 3-7, edited)

And, within the third and fourth lines of the fourth paragraph on page 55, they summarize the spiritual journey of recovery in four words: **". . . search diligently within yourself. . . ."**

These are dramatic and for some of us revolutionary concepts. Let us summarize them for you. First, the authors of the "Big Book" announce they have found a way to free us from the bondage of addictive or compulsive behaviors. Next, they describe the solution as a **"Power greater than ourselves."** Then, they tell us where we find this Power—right inside each and every one of us.

Now we know **WHERE** to find this Power. Much of the rest of the "Big Book" is devoted to the question of **HOW** to find this Power.

Basically, we become empowered by taking the Twelve Steps. The Steps are described in depth and detail in the "Big Book."

We have provided you with a list of the Twelve Steps along with the page numbers where each Step is located. We've also included the specific passage within each Step that contains the directions for taking that Step.

(Refer participants to the handout titled, "Suggested 'Big Book' Passages for Taking the Twelve Steps".)

Let's begin with the First Step. It reads:

We admitted we (had a problem)–that our lives had

become unmanageable.

In order to recover, we must make a surrender. The "Big Book" authors devote 51 pages of the book to the first part of the surrender process which is to admit we have a problem.

In the first chapter of the "Big Book," titled, "Bill's Story," Bill W., describes how he made his surrender. In addition, he tells us how he took the rest of the Steps and recovered.

In the first seven pages of his story, Bill describes the progressive nature of his illness. In the 1920's, he was a successful Wall Street stock analyst. In a few short years he loses everything.

In the first paragraph on page 8, Bill has a moment of clarity. He realizes he is powerless over alcohol. He is licked--defeated:

> "No words can tell of the loneliness and despair I found in that bitter morass of self-pity. Quicksand stretched around me in all directions. I had met my match. I had been overwhelmed. . . ."
>
> (pg. 8, para. 1, lines 1-4)

But, Bill cannot stop drinking on this admission alone. In late November 1934, Bill is visited by an old high school friend, Ebby T. Bill is drunk. Ebby has been sober for several months. When Bill asks Ebby how he stopped drinking, Ebby tells him that all he did was take a few simple Steps. Bill is shocked but he lets Ebby continue because, as he writes, **"my gin would last longer than his preaching."**

Soon after Ebby's visit, Bill checks into Towns Hospital. There, under the direction of Dr. Silkworth, Bill is physically withdrawn from alcohol for the fourth time.

While in the hospital, Bill takes the equivalent of the Twelve Steps as we know them today. With Ebby as his sharing partner, he completes the Steps in one or two days. Not one or two months or one or two years, but one or two days. This is how Bill describes his recovery.

In the second paragraph on page 13, Bill makes a complete **SURRENDER:**

> "There I humbly offered myself to God, as I then understood (God), to (lead and guide) me. I placed myself unreservedly under (God's) care and direction. . . ."
>
> (pg. 13, para. 2, lines 1-3, edited)

Immediately after his Surrender, Bill begins **SHARING** his shortcomings with Ebby. Starting with the second line in the second paragraph on page 13, Bill writes:

> ". . . I ruthlessly faced my (shortcomings) and became willing to have my newfound Friend take them away, root and branch. . . .
>
> "My schoolmate visited me, and I fully acquainted him with my problems and deficiencies. . . ."
>
> (pg. 13, para. 2, lines 5-7; para. 3, lines 1-2, edited)

Together, Bill and Ebby identify the blocks that were preventing Bill from tapping into the Power greater than human power–the Power that would solve his problem. Then, starting with the second line in the third paragraph on page 13, Bill learns how to remove the blocks by making **AMENDS**:

> ". . . We made a list of people I had hurt or toward whom I felt resentment. I expressed my entire willingness to approach these individuals, admitting my wrong. Never was I to be critical of them. I was to right all such matters to the utmost of my ability."
>
> (pg. 13, para. 3, lines 2-7)

In the fourth paragraph on page 13, Bill gets quiet, listens to the indwelling spirit, and follows **GUIDANCE.** These actions are essential for establishing a two-way relationship with the **"One who has all power"**:

> "I was to test my thinking by the new God-consciousness within. Common sense would thus become uncommon sense. I was to sit quietly when in doubt, asking only for direction and strength to meet my problems as (God) would have me. . . ."
>
> (pg. 13, para. 4, lines 1-5, edited)

Bill then has a **"psychic change."** In the second paragraph on page 14, Bill describes his spiritual awakening:

> "These were revolutionary and drastic proposals, but the moment I fully accepted them, the effect was electric. There was a sense of victory, followed by such a peace and serenity as I had never known. There was

> utter confidence. I felt lifted up, as though the great clean wind of a mountain top blew through and through. God comes to most (people) gradually, but (God's) impact on me was sudden and profound."
>
> (pg. 14, para. 2, lines 1-8, edited)

Bill made direct contact with the **"Spirit of the Universe"** and overcame his problem.

There is additional material within these 51 pages of the "Big Book" that further explains our physical and mental symptoms and how our lives have become unmanageable as the result of our self-destructive behaviors. All we've done is highlight some of the more important passages. However, we hope we've shown you enough for you to proceed.

Now, it's time for us to begin our journey toward the spiritual awakening that will change our lives. Let's see who is ready to take the First Step? Again, it reads:

We admitted we (had a problem)—that our lives had become unmanageable.

The "Big Book" authors tell us exactly what we have to do. In the second paragraph on page 30, they write:

> "We learned that we had to fully concede to our innermost selves that we (have a problem). This is the first step in recovery. The delusion that we are like other people, or presently may be, has to be smashed."
>
> (pg. 30, para. 2, lines 1-4, edited)

Maybe your only problem is that your life is a bit out of control. If this is the case, you can take the First Step based on unmanageability. In the second paragraph on page 52, starting with the third line, we learn some of the characteristics of unmanageability:

> ". . . We were having trouble with personal relationships, we couldn't control our emotional natures, we were (suffering from) misery and depression, . . . we had a feeling of uselessness, we were full of fear, we were unhappy, we couldn't seem to be of real help to other people . . ."
>
> (pg. 52, para. 2, lines 3-8, edited)

We have converted these statements into questions. If you can answer "yes" to any of them, please raise your hand. If you've been in recovery for awhile, please think back to when you first got here. Okay let's begin.

(Ask the questions.)

1. Are you having trouble with personal relationships? (Ask for a show of hands.)
2. Are you having difficulty controlling your emotional nature? (Again, ask for a show of hands.)
3. Do you suffer from misery and depression? (Anyone?)
4. Do you have feelings of uselessness? (Okay, hands up.)
5. Are you full of fear?
6. Are you unhappy?
7. Does it seem like you can't be of real help to other peo-

ple?

According to the "Big Book" authors, those who raised their hands, in response to any of these questions, are ready to take Step One.

Now, let's answer the First Step question in unison. All that is needed is a "yes" or "no" reply. This is the First Step question:

"Do you concede to your innermost self that you have a problem?"

And, your answer is?

(Have the participants answer the First Step question.)

Thank you. According to the "Big Book" authors, those who answered "yes" to this question have taken Step One.

Now, let's move on to the Second Step, which reads:

Came to believe that a Power greater than our-selves could restore us to sanity.

Now that we have admitted we have a problem, let's look at what we have to do to in order to overcome this problem. According to the "Big Book" authors, we have to tap into **"the realm of the spirit," "a source of power much greater than (ourselves)"** that will free us from the bondage of our self-destructive behaviors.

In the middle of page 46, the authors ask us to set aside any contempt we might have for spiritual principles and consider our own concept of a Power greater than human power–a pow-er that resides inside each of us. If we do, we will be in a much better position to understand the spiritual solution the "Big Book" authors are talking about. Starting with the third line in the first paragraph, they state:

> ". . . We found that as soon as we were able to lay aside prejudice and express even a willingness to believe in a Power greater than ourselves, we commenced to get results, even though it was impossible for any of us to fully define or comprehend that Power . . ."
>
> (pg. 46, para. 1, lines 3-8)

Basically, the "Big Book" authors tell us it is impossible to fully comprehend the **"Power of God."** We have to stop trying to grasp this Power with our mind and start accepting this Power with our heart. In the first paragraph on page 47, they explain the concept of **"God as you understand God."**:

> "When, therefore, we speak to you of God, we mean your own conception of God. This applies, too, to other spiritual expressions which you find in this book. Do not let any prejudice you may have against spiritual terms deter you from honestly asking yourself what they mean to you. At the start, this was all we needed to commence spiritual growth, to effect our first conscious relation with God as we understood (God). . . . (I)f we wished to grow we had to begin somewhere. So, we used our own conception, however

limited it was."

(pg. 47, para. 1, lines 1-9, 11-13, edited)

Once again we need to make a decision. We have to decide whether or not we believe in an indwelling Spirit—a **"God-consciousness within."** In the second paragraph on page 53, the "Big Book" authors write

> "When we became . . . crushed by a self-imposed crisis we could not postpone or evade, we had to fear-essly face the proposition that either God is every-thing or else (God) is nothing. God either is, or (God) isn't. What was our choice to be?"
>
> (pg. 53, para. 2, lines 1-5, edited)

Now, it's time to choose. Are we willing to concede that there is a **"Power greater than ourselves?"** If we are, we're ready to take the Second Step.

In the second paragraph on page 47, we find the directions:

> "We needed to ask ourselves but one short question. 'Do I now believe, or am I even willing to believe, that there is a Power greater than myself?' As soon as (someone says) that (they do) believe, or (are) will ing to believe, we emphatically assure (them) that (they are on their) way. It has been repeatedly proven among us that upon this simple cornerstone a wonderfully effective spiritual structure can be built."
>
> (pg. 47, para. 2, lines 1-8, edited)

Let's see who is ready to proceed? We ask that you answer the Second Step question, in unison, with a "yes" or "no reply. This is the question:

"Do you now believe, or are you even willing to believe, that there is a Power greater than yourself?"

And, your answer is?

(Have the participants answer the Second Step question)

Thank you. According to the "Big Book" authors, those who answered "yes" to this question have taken Step Two.

Now, let's look at the Third Step, which reads:

Made a decision to turn our will and our lives over to the care of God <u>as we understood (God)</u>.

Even though we may believe that the **"Power of God"** is the answer to our problems, this doesn't necessarily mean we are willing to implement this solution. In order to recover, we must make a decision to put this Power to work in our lives.

On pages 62 and 63, the "Big Book" authors show us how to become God directed. But, first they tell us how being self-directed keeps us separated from the spiritual solution to our difficulties.

In the first paragraph on page 62, the authors declare that it is our selfishness and self-centeredness that gets us into trouble.

We need to take responsibility for this excessive self-interest and self-absorption and ask God to remove this shortcoming from our lives:

> "Selfishness—self-centeredness! That, we think, is the root of our troubles. Driven by a hundred forms of fear, self-delusion, self-seeking, and self-pity, we step on the toes of our fellows and they retaliate. Sometimes they hurt us, seemingly without provocation, but we invariably find that at some time in the past we have made decisions based on self which later placed us in a position to be hurt.
>
> "So our troubles, we think, are basically of our own making. They arise out of ourselves and (we are) an extreme example of self-will run riot, though (we) usually (don't) think so. Above everything, we . . . must be rid of this selfishness. We must, or it kills us! God makes that possible. And there often seems no way of entirely getting rid of self without (God's) aid. . . ."
>
> (pg. 62, para. 1, lines 1-8; para. 2, lines 1-8, edited)

Then in the third paragraph on page 62, the authors tell us what happens once we rid ourselves of this selfishness:

> "This is the how and why of it. First of all, we had to quit playing God. It didn't work. Next, we decided that hereafter in this drama of life, God was going to be our Director. . . .
>
> "When we sincerely took such a position, all sorts of remarkable things followed, We had a new Employer.

> Being all powerful, (God) provided what we needed, if we kept close . . . and performed (God's) work well. . . ."
>
> (pg. 62, para. 3, lines 1-4; p. 63, para. 1, lines 1-4, edited)

Now we know our place in God's universe. Contrary to what we may have thought in the past, the whole world does not revolve around us.

Realizing there is a **"Power greater than ourselves"** is the essence of God Consciousness. As we become aware of the **"realm of the spirit,"** our lives change. We begin to **"lose our fear of today, tomorrow or the hereafter."**

It is decision time once again. The "Big Book" authors state we are now ready to take the Third Step. They even provide us with a prayer we can use to take this Step. The prayer is in the middle of page 63, starting with the second line in the second paragraph. We would like each of you who is ready to take the Third Step to read this prayer along with us. Are we ready? Okay, let's begin:

> ". . . God, I offer myself to Thee—to build with me and to do with me as Thou wilt. Relieve me of the bondage of self, that I may better do Thy will. Take away my difficulties, that victory over them may bear witness to those I would help of Thy Power, Thy Love, and Thy Way of life. May I do Thy will always!"
>
> (pg. 63, para. 2, lines 2-8)

According to the "Big Book" authors, we have taken Step

Three.

That's enough for this session. In the past hour, we have covered 71 pages of the "Big Book" and taken the first three Steps. This is a remarkable achievement. Congratulations.

During the next meeting we will provide you with guidelines for taking the Fourth and Fifth Steps. You will fill out a Fourth Step inventory and discuss it with your sharing partner between the second and the third sessions.

Are there any questions?

Chapter 2

Session #2–Steps 4 and 5

WELCOME to the second session of ***Back to the Basics of Recovery.*** Together, we are taking the Twelve Steps based on the directions found in the "Big Book" and the personal experiences of the Twelve-step pioneers.

Our names are ___________ and ___________, and we will be your guides for this meeting. During this session we will take Step Four and make preparations for Step Five.

We will use a simple assets and liabilities checklist to identify the personality traits that have kept us "shut . . . off from the sunlight of the Spirit." By ridding ourselves of these shortcomings, we will expand our **"consciousness of the power of God in our lives."**

Step Four Reads:

Made a searching and fearless moral inventory of ourselves.

In the fourth paragraph on page 63, the "Big Book" authors tell us what we need to do now that we've made our decision to proceed

> "Next we launched out on a course of vigorous action, the first step of which is a personal housecleaning, which many of us had never attempted. Though our

decision was a vital and crucial step, it could have little permanent effect unless at once followed by a strenuous effort to face, and to be rid of, the things in ourselves which had been blocking us. Our (self-destructive behavior) was but a symptom. So we had to get down to causes and conditions."

(pg. 63, para. 4, lines 1-2; pg. 64, lines 1-7, edited)

Please note the authors say **AT ONCE.** They instruct us to take the Fourth Step immediately after the Third Step prayer. We must identify and remove those things that have been blocking us from the spiritual solution to our difficulties.

The "Big Book" authors start by comparing a personal inventory to a business inventory. In the first paragraph on page 64, they state:

> "Therefore we started upon a personal inventory. *This was Step Four.* A business which takes no regular inventory usually goes broke. Taking a commercial inventory is a fact-finding and fact-facing process. It is an effort to discover the truth about the stock-in-trade. One object is to disclose damaged or unsalable goods, to get rid of them promptly and without regret."
>
> (pg. 64, para. 1, lines 1-7)

So, we are going to conduct the equivalent of a commercial inventory on our lives. What is a commercial inventory? For those who have taken an accounting class either in high school or college, we learned that the equation for double-entry bookkeeping is: **Assets = Liabilities + Owner Equity.** So, according to the "Big Book" authors we are going to look at our assets and liabilities. That's what a commercial inventory is all about. It's an examination of what is working and what is not working in our lives. It provides us with the opportunity to accentuate the positive and eliminate the negative.

Then, in the second paragraph on page 64, the authors clearly explain what we need to do in order to conduct a commercial inventory:

> "We did exactly the same thing with our lives. We took stock honestly. First, we searched out the flaws in our make-up which caused our failure. Being convinced that self, manifested in various ways, was what had defeated us, we considered its common manifestations."
>
> (pg. 64, para. 2, lines 1-6)

So, the "Big Book" authors ask us to start with the liabilities side of the ledger. First, we look at our shortcomings.

Before we get into the details on how to take this Step, we want to emphasize a few things. First, there is no right or wrong way to take a commercial inventory. There are several assets and liabilities checklists in use today. You can use any one of them.

Second, the commercial inventory described on page 64 precedes a three-column example described on page 65. Because this examination of our assets and liabilities comes first, we assume the "Big Book" authors are asking us to utilize this simple checklist before attempting the more difficult inventory on the following page.

Fourth Step Inventory

Assets and Liabilities Checklist from the "Big Book"
pg. 64:1(1-7); pg. 64:3(1-9); pg. 68:1(1-3); pg. 69:1(1-6:edited)

Liabilities Watch for—		**Assets** Strive for—
Resentment		Forgiveness
Fear		Faith
Selfishness		Unselfishness
Dishonesty		Honesty
False Pride		Humility
Jealousy		Trust
Envy		Contentment
Laziness		Action

Assets and Liabilities Checklist

Third, Dr. Bob, a Twelve-Step pioneer from the 1930's and 1940's, used an assets and liabilities checklist to take thousands of people through the Fourth Step. Dr. Bob believed that, initially, newcomers should be taken through a simplified version of the inventory process. Later, they can work the Step in more detail.

We have provided everyone with an example of the assets and liabilities checklist that was used by many of the pioneers. It is the same format as the one published in the June 1946 issue of a recovery newsletter.

All we have done is remove some of the vertical lines, so we can list the people, institutions and principles we need to talk about to the right of the appropriate liabilities.

We are now going to define these liabilities in order to provide a clearer understanding of their meaning.

RESENTMENT is the consequence of being angry or bitter toward someone for an extended period of time over some real or imagined insult. It is a hostile or indignant attitude in response to an alleged affront or personal injury.

FEAR is being afraid of losing something we have or not getting something we want. It manifests itself in many ways such as phobia, terror, panic, anxiety and worry.

SELFISHNESS is concern only for ourselves, our own welfare or pleasure, without regard for, or at the expense of, others.

DISHONESTY involves theft or deception. It includes taking things that don't belong to us, cheating people out of what

Fourth Step Inventory

Assets and Liabilities Checklist from the "Big Book"
pg. 64:1(1-7); pg. 64:3(1-9); pg. 68:1(1-3); pg. 69:1(1-6:edited)

Liabilities
Watch for—

Resentment	*Ex*	*Myself*	*Court*	*God*
Fear	*Court*	*Relapse*	*Health*	
Selfishness	*Ex*	*Employer*	*Friend #1*	
Dishonesty	*Ex*	*Myself*	*Employer*	*Friend #2*
False Pride	*God*	*Employer*		
Jealousy	*Family Member*			
Envy				
Laziness	*Ex*	*Employer*	*Myself*	
Shame	*Friend #2*			

Example of Assets and Liabilities Checklist After Answering Questions

is rightfully theirs, and lying to or withholding the truth from others.

FALSE PRIDE is either feeling better than or less than someone else. Feelings of superiority include prejudice about race, education or religious beliefs; and sarcasm–putting someone else down to make us feel better about ourselves. Feelings of inferiority include self-pity–dwelling on one's own problems, and low self-esteem–the lack of self-worth or self-respect.

JEALOUSY has to do with people being suspicious of another's motives or doubting the faithfulness of a friend.

ENVY has to do with things–wanting someone else's possessions.

LAZINESS means lacking the will or the desire to work. Procrastination, which is postponing or delaying an assigned job or task, is a form of laziness.

Dr. Bob used this format to take newcomers through the Steps as quickly as possible. In many instances, he completed the process during a person's three-to-five day stay at St. Thomas hospital in Akron, Ohio. Today, many millions have recovered by following Dr. Bob's "keep it simple" approach.

The "Big Book" authors also urge us to take the Steps quickly. We must discover **"the truth about the stock-in-trade"** in order to remove those behaviors that have cut us off from the **"sunlight of the Spirit."** In the third paragraph on page 65, the authors provide us with some of the details:

"We went back through our lives. Nothing counted but thoroughness and honesty. When we were finished we considered it carefully. . . ."

(pg. 65, para.3, lines 1-3)

Please note that the authors ask us to be thorough and, in the very next sentence, they tell us what to do when we are finished. Since this is all in one paragraph, we assume they are asking us to complete this inventory in one sitting.

Keep in mind this is only a suggestion. You can spend as much time on this inventory as you wish, just as long as you discuss it with your sharing partner before the next session.

Now, let's look at what we put on paper. From pages 64 to 71, the authors present us with a list of liabilities we need to eliminate and assets we need to accentuate. In the third paragraph on page 64, they ask us to examine our resentments:

"Resentment is the 'number one' offender. It destroys more (of us) than anything else. From it stem all forms of spiritual disease . . . . . . In dealing with resentments, we set them on paper. We listed people, institutions or principles with whom we were angry. . . ."

(pg. 64, para. 3, lines 1-3, 6-9, edited)

Then, in the second paragraph on page 67, the authors instruct us to look for our own mistakes to see if we need to make amends:

"Referring to our list again. Putting out of our minds

> the wrongs others had done, we resolutely looked for our own mistakes. Where had we been selfish, dishonest, self-seeking and frightened? Though a situation had not been entirely our fault, we tried to disregard the other person involved entirely. Where were we to blame? The inventory was ours, not the other (person's). When we saw our faults we listed them. We placed them before us in black and white. We admitted our wrongs honestly and were willing to set these matters straight."
>
> (pg. 67, para. 2, lines 1-11, edited)

To see where we were at fault regarding the incidents and events on our checklist can be both revealing and healing. To stop blaming others and take responsibility for our actions can result in a **"revolutionary change in (our) way of living and thinking."**

Let's look at the third sentence in this paragraph again. It reads, **"Where had we been selfish, dishonest, self-seeking and frightened?"** These shortcomings are based on self-will. In addition, they are the opposites of unselfish, honest, forgiving and faithful, which are some of the characteristics of God's will.

We can use this test for self-will vs. God's will to determine if we need to **"set right the wrong"** by making amends:

Test for self-will	Test for God's will
Selfish	**Unselfish**
Dishonest	**Honest**
Self-seeking	**Forgiving**
Frightened	**Faithful**

Regarding our resentments, the "Big Book" authors provide us with specific instructions on what we are to do. We must get beyond them if we **"expect to live long or happily in this world."**

In the third paragraph on page 66, the authors explain that when we hold onto grudges, we are actually allowing others to control our lives.

> "We turned back to our list, for it held the key to the future. We were prepared to look at it from an entirely different angle. We began to see that the world and its people really dominated us. In that state, the wrong-doing of others, fancied or real, had power to actually kill. How could we escape? We saw that these resentments must be mastered, but how? . . ."
>
> (pg. 66, para. 3, lines 1-7)

If we don't deal with our resentments, the future will just be a repeat of the past. Each time we are reminded of an old hurt, the old pain returns and we feel it again and again. In the past we may have engaged in self-destructive behaviors to numb this pain, but now we are going to take the actions necessary to relieve this pain.

The first thing we do is discuss our resentments with our sharing partner or partners. The healing process starts when we talk about the hurt. But, we cannot fully recover until we forgive those who have offended us. We overcome resentment with forgiveness.

We must change our attitude about the experience. We do

this by seeing the source of our pain in a new light. We see the person as a sick individual, who need our prayers not our anger. Whether it is a person who is still in our lives, someone who has passed on, someone we may never see again, or ourselves, the process is the same. We must forgive. Starting with the first line on page 67, the "Big Book" authors write:

> "Though we did not like their symptoms and the way these disturbed us, they, like ourselves, were sick too. We asked God to help us show them the same tolerance, pity, and patience that we would cheerfully grant a sick friend. When (someone) offended we said to ourselves, 'This is a sick (person). How can I be helpful . . . ? God save me from being angry. Thy will be done.'
>
> "We avoid retaliation or argument. We wouldn't treat sick people that way. If we do, we destroy our chance of being helpful. We cannot be helpful to all people, but at least God will show us how to take a kindly and tolerant view of each and every one."
>
> (pg. 67, lines 1-8; para. 1, lines 1-5, edited)

Now, it is time to begin the Fourth Step by making a list of resentments. We realize that the sharing partners are supposed to work on this list together, but if you would like to get a head start on the sharing process, you can start filling out a checklist right now. This way you can discuss your inventory as soon as we close this session. For those who are uncertain or hesitant about doing this, your sharing partner will ask the questions and fill out the sheet for you when you get together.

In the open space to the right of the word, "Resentment," we write down the people, institutions and principles with whom we are angry. We record the first two or three names that come to mind.

To protect our anonymity, we write down the generic equivalents of the specific names of those we are inventorying. For example, instead of, "Susan" we can write, "Family Member" and instead of, "Bill," we can write, "Friend Number One."

We deal with the resentments that are bothering us right now. In the days ahead, we will conduct additional inventories to take care of those things that may still be troubling us then.

Our objective is to immediately get to the **"causes and conditions"** that are currently blocking us from God and our fellows. We do this by making amends to those we've harmed and forgiving those who have harmed us.

(Take a few minutes so everyone can work on their Resentment List.)

Next, the authors ask us to look at our fears. In the first paragraph on page 68, they write:

> "We reviewed our fears thoroughly. We put them on paper, even though we had no resentment in connection with them. We asked ourselves why we had them. Wasn't it because self-reliance failed us? Self-reliance was good as far as it went, but it didn't go far enough. Some of us once had great self-confidence, but it didn't fully solve the fear problem, or any other."
>
> (pg. 68, para. 1, lines 1-7)

In the third paragraph on page 68, the "Big Book" authors inform us that we will lose our fears if we have faith in the **"Power of God":**

> ". . . We can laugh at those who think spirituality the way of weakness. Paradoxically, it is the way of strength. The verdict of the ages is that faith means courage. All (people) of faith have courage. They trust their God. We never apologize for God. Instead we let (God) demonstrate, through us, what (God) can do. We ask (God) to remove our fear and direct our attention to what (God) would have us be. At once, we commence to outgrow fear."
>
> (pg. 68, para. 3, lines 2-10, edited)

Now, it is time to make a Fear list. Let's start with those fears that have **"no resentment in connection with them."** To the right of the word, "Fear," we write down the people, institutions or principles that have caused us to be afraid.

Then we look back over our "Resentment" list. If, in addition to anger, we have fear or a phobia regarding someone or something, we write down the generic equivalent of the person or the thing we are afraid of to the right of "Fear."

(Take a few minutes so everyone can work on their Fear List.)

In the first paragraph on page 69, the authors mention some additional shortcomings we need to address:

> "We reviewed our own conduct over the years past.

> Where had we been selfish, dishonest or inconsiderate? Whom had we hurt? Did we unjustifiably arouse jealousy, suspicion or bitterness. Where were we at fault, what should we have done instead? We got this all down on paper and looked at it."
>
> (pg. 69, para. 1, lines 1-6)

We overcome harms with amends. The Big Book authors confirm this in the third paragraph on page 69, starting with the second line:

> ". . . We must be willing to make amends where we have done harm, provided that we do not bring about still more harm in so doing. . . ."
>
> (pg. 69, para. 3, lines 2-4)

Now, it is time to make a Harms list. According to the "Big Book" authors we need to look at our "Selfishness," "Dishonesty," "Inconsideration," "Jealousy," "Suspicion" and "Bitterness." On the checklist list we have provided you, we have substituted "False Pride" for "Inconsideration," "Envy" for "Suspicion" and "Laziness" for "Bitterness." These liabilities come from the June 1946 issue of a recovery newsletter.

If we have hurt anyone, we put their name to the right of the harm that applies. Then we check to see if resentment and/or fear also apply.

(Take a few minutes so everyone can work on their Harms List.)

So much for the liabilities side of the ledger. Now, what

about the assets?

The "Big Book" authors list assets throughout Chapter 5. We've already explained that the asset that corresponds to the liability of "Resentment" is **"FORGIVENESS"** and the asset that corresponds to the liability of "fear" is **"FAITH."** Additional assets that correspond to the remainder of the liabilities are **"UNSELFISHNESS," "HONESTY," "HUMILITY," "TRUST," "CONTENTMENT,"** and **"ACTION."**

We have now looked at both sides of the ledger. Our inventory consists of a list of liabilities to watch for and assets to strive for.

Keep in mind that it is not necessary to talk about every resentment, selfish act, or person you have ever lied to in order for the inventory to be thorough. The objective is to get to **"causes and conditions"** Sometimes it takes only a few incidents to make clear which shortcomings have kept us blocked from an intimate, two-way relationship with the **"One who has all power."**

In the process of sharing our inventory, we may find that we need to **"set right the wrong."** If that is the case, we circle the name of the person, organization or principle that needs to be addressed. The circled names become our Eighth Step amends list.

After we have finished talking about the events or circumstances represented by the names to the right of the "Liabilities," we unfold the checklist so we can look at the Assets side of the sheet. The sharing partner will usually end the session by

Fourth Step Inventory

Assets and Liabilities Checklist from the "Big Book"
pg. 64:1(1-7); pg. 64:3(1-9); pg. 68:1(1-3); pg. 69:1(1-6:edited)

Liabilities Watch for—					Assets Strive for—
Resentment	*Ex*	*Myself*	*Court*	*God*	Forgiveness
Fear	*Court*	*Relapse*	*Health*		Faith
Selfishness	*Ex*	*Employer*	(*Friend #1*)		Unselfishness
Dishonesty	(*Ex*)	*Myself*	(*Employer*)	(*Friend #2*)	Honesty
False Pride	*God*	*Employer*			Humility
Jealousy	(*Family Member*)				Trust
Envy					Contentment
Laziness	(*Ex*)	*Employer*	(*Myself*)		Action
Shame	*Friend #2*				*Self-respect*

Example of Assets and Liabilities Checklist with Eight Step Amends List describing the Assets we already have (those with the least number of **NAMES**) and the Assets that will be strengthened (those with the most number of **NAMES**) as we make our amends.

To see how this is done, let's look at the handout subtitled, "Checklist with Eight Step Amends List." Using this example as a guide, please follow along as I summarize the sharing session for this person. Based on the **NAMES** on this sheet, I would say something like, "This inventory shows that, for the most part, you are a humble, trusting, and contented person with considerable self-respect. In addition, you will become more forgiving and loving as you let bygones be bygones, and you will become more unselfish, honest, and industrious as you make amends for your selfishness, dishonesty, and laziness."

The Liabilities with **NAMES** to the right of them are the shortcomings we turn over to God in Steps Six and Seven. As mentioned previously, the circled **NAMES** are our Eighth Step amends list.

Next to the circles, we can add **NOTES** to identify the specific type of amends we are to make in Step Nine. The Amends mentioned in the "Big Book" are: "Direct Amends," "Living Amends," "Amends-in-Kind," and "Amends to Those Who Cannot be Seen." We'll talk more about the amends process next session.

So, on one sheet of paper, we now have everything we need to take Steps Four, Five, Six, Seven, Eight and Nine.

We look at assets as well as liabilities because many of us have lost much of our self-esteem and self-worth as the result of our addictive or compulsive behaviors. Even though we've done some very foolish and destructive things, we will never have to repeat those actions, provided we are willing to admit our faults and correct them. If we are genuinely sorry, God has already forgiven us. Now, we need to forgive ourselves.

So, it is time to make a searching and fearless moral inventory. As a result of doing this, we will clean up the wreckage of the past so we can strengthen our connection with the **"Spirit of the Universe."**

We have completed our presentation on the Fourth Step, but before we end this session, we need to discuss one more detail—the person or persons with whom we share our inventory.

Step Five reads:

"Admitted to God, to ourselves, and to another human being the exact nature of our wrongs."

On page 72, starting with the ninth line in the second paragraph, the "Big Book" authors tell us why we need to admit our faults to another person:

> ". . . The best reason first: If we skip this vital step, we may not overcome (our difficulties). Time after time newcomers have tried to keep to themselves certain facts about their lives. Trying to avoid this humbling experience, they have turned to easier methods. Almost invariably they (relapsed). Having persevered with the rest of the program, they wondered why they fell. We think the reason is that they never completed their housecleaning. They took inventory all right, but

> hung on to some of the worst items in stock. . . ."
>
> (pg. 72, para. 2, lines 9-13; pg. 73, lines 1-5, edited)

Since we're not good judges of character, especially our own, we confide in someone else. Only another person can see us as we really are.

This individual can be the member of the Twelve-step community who is helping you through these sessions, but it doesn't have to be. The "Big Book" authors provide us with other options.

Starting with the fourth paragraph on page 73, they give us directions on how to choose the person or persons with whom we share our inventories.:

> "We must be entirely honest with somebody if we expcct to live long or happily in this world. Rightly and naturally, we think well before we choose the person or persons with whom to take this intimate and confidential step. . . . . . .Though we have no religious connection, we may still do well to talk with someone ordained by an established religion. . . .
>
> "If we cannot or would rather not do this, we search our acquaintance for a close-mouthed, understanding friend. Perhaps our doctor or psychologist will be the person. . . ."
>
> (pg. 73, para. 4, line 1; pg. 74, lines 1-4, 7-9; para. 1, lines 1-4, edited)

Of critical importance is confidentiality. The "Big Book" authors list some of the people who are legally bound to keep a secret. This "privilege" protects communications between certain individuals and insures that these communications will remain confidential. The people listed in the "Big Book" who have this legal protection are religious, medical, and mental health professionals. Attorneys also have this "privilege."

This "privilege" is not absolute–there are exceptions. This legal protection does not include Twelve-step sponsors or sharing partners. This is why we must be very careful about what we share during a Fifth Step.

If you feel uncomfortable talking about some parts of your checklist with your partner, all we ask is that you make a commitment to this person as to when, where, and with whom you will share those portions of your inventory.

If you are willing to make this commitment, you can take the rest of the Steps with us today. In the second paragraph on page 74, the "Big Book" authors explain the circumstances under which this Step may be temporarily postponed:

> "Notwithstanding the great necessity for discussing ourselves with someone, it may be one is so situated that there is no suitable person available. If that is so, this step may be postponed, only, however, if we hold ourselves in complete readiness to go through with it at the first opportunity. . . ."
>
> (pg. 74, para. 2, lines 1-6)

The "Big Book" authors give us specific instructions for taking the Fifth Step. In the first paragraph on page 75, they tell us that, as soon as we decide who we are going to talk to, we take action immediately:

> "When we decide who is to hear our story, we waste no time. We have a written inventory and we are prepared for a long talk. We explain to our partner what we are about to do and why we have to do it. (Our partner) should realize that we are engaged upon a life-and-death errand. Most people approached this way will be glad to help; they will be honored by our confidence."
>
> (pg. 75, para. 1, lines 1-8, edited)

Then, the "Big Book" authors announce that, once we admit our shortcomings, our lives will change. On page 75, starting with the second line in the second paragraph, they describe some of these changes:

> ". . .Once we have taken this step, withholding nothing, we are delighted. We can look the world in the eye. We can be alone at perfect peace and ease. Our fears fall from us. We begin to feel the nearness of our Creator. We may have had certain spiritual beliefs, but now we begin to have a spiritual experience. The feeling that (our) problem has disappeared will often come strongly. We feel we are on the Broad Highway, walking hand in hand with the Spirit of the Universe."
>
> (pg. 75, para. 2, lines 2-11, edited)

We are now well on our way toward recovering from our addictive and compulsive behaviors. The authors tell us we are in the process of having a spiritual experience. As the result of this **"psychic change,"** our obsessions are being removed.

Please, let the **"God-consciousness within"** guide you through the inventory process. If you do, you'll find these steps simple and straightforward.

As we have already said, there is no right or wrong way to do the Fourth and Fifth Steps. Just do them.

Are there any questions?

Chapter 3

Session #3–Steps 6, 7, 8 and 9

WELCOME to session number three of ***Back to the Basics of Recovery.*** Together, we're taking the Twelve Steps as described in the "Big Book." Our objective is to take the actions necessary to free us from our addictive or compulsive behaviors.

Our names are ___________ and ___________, and we will be your guides for this meeting. During this session we will take Steps Six, Seven, Eight and Nine.

During the past two sessions, we have taken Steps One through Four. Between sessions two and three, we shared our Fourth Step with our sharing partner. Hopefully, during this talk, we learned about our strengths and weaknesses and **"admitted our wrongs honestly and were willing to set these matters straight."**

We will turn our shortcomings over to God, as we understand God, in Steps Six and Seven. Then, we will make amends to those we've harmed, and forgive those who have harmed us, in Steps Eight and Nine.

We are entering the phase of the program where more and more actions are required. These actions produce results. Many of these results are in the form of promises which, as our lives change, become an integral part of our spiritual being.

Please keep in mind that recovery offers so much more than just freedom from addictive and compulsive behaviors. We have found a new way of living far more beautiful than anything we ever could have imagined. That's why we take the Steps, and that's why we take them again and again.

Let's proceed to the Sixth Step. It reads:

Were entirely ready to have God remove all these defects of character.

In this Step, the "Big Book" authors have us answer a simple question. On page 76, starting with the third line in the first paragraph, they ask:

> ". . . Are we now ready to let God remove from us all the things which we have admitted are objectionable? Can (God) now take them all—every one? If we still cling to something we will not let go, we ask God to help us be willing."
>
> ("Big Book," pg. 76, para.1, lines 3-7, edited)

So, according to the "Big Book" authors, it is decision time once again. We realize they want us to take our Sixth Step right after we share our Fourth Step with our sharing partner. In case this person didn't direct you to page 76 of the "Big Book," we'll take you there now. If you have already taken the Sixth Step, we ask you to take it again now with the Group.

During the Fifth Step, we identified our shortcomings using an assets and liabilities checklist we described last session. In Step Six, we make the preparations necessary to turn these shortcomings over to the **"One who has all power."**

Let's start with a moment of silence so we can ask God to remove the liabilities that we found were blocking us when we shared our inventory.

(Observe one to two minutes of silence)

Now, let's take the Sixth Step together. We ask that you answer the Sixth Step question, in unison, with a "yes" or "no reply. This is the question:

"Are you now ready to let God remove from you all the things which you have admitted are objectionable?"

And, your answer is?

(Have the participants answer the Sixth Step question.)

Thank you.

According to the "Big Book" authors, those who answered "yes" to this question have taken Step Six and are ready to move on to the Seventh Step, which reads:

Humbly asked (God) to remove our shortcomings.

This Step is straightforward. It consists of a prayer in which we ask God to remove our liabilities and strengthen our assets so we can be of maximum service to all.

The prayer is found in the second paragraph on page 76. For

those who are ready, let's read the Seventh Step prayer together. Okay, let's begin:

> ". . . My Creator, I am now willing that you should have all of me, good and bad. I pray that you now remove from me every single defect of character which stands in the way of my usefulness to you and my fellows. Grant me strength, as I go out from here, to do your bidding. . . ."
>
> (pg. 76, para. 2, lines 1-7)

According to the "Big Book" authors, we have taken Step Seven

Now, it is time to clear away the wreckage of our past. We do this by making amends to those we have harmed and forgiving those who have harmed us.

Step Eight reads:

Made a list of all persons we had harmed, and became willing to make amends to them all.

The "Big Book" authors state, **"made a list."** Do we need to make this list? Actually, no! We compiled our list as part of our Fourth and Fifth Steps. In the third paragraph on page 76, the "Big Book" authors confirm this:

> "Now we need more action, without which we find that 'Faith without works is dead.' Let's look at *Steps*

> *Eight and Nine.* We have a list of all persons we have harmed and to whom we are willing to make amends. We made it when we took inventory. . . ."
>
> (pg. 76, para. 3, lines 1-5)

That's why we hold onto our Fourth Step inventory. It contains our Eighth Step amends list. Using our assets and liabilities checklist, the amends are the names on the sheet that are circled.

Let's move on to the Ninth Step, which reads:

Made direct amends to such people, wherever possible, except when to do so would injure them or others.

The amends process is explained in detail on pages 76 through 83 of the "Big Book." On page 76, starting with the sixth line in the third paragraph, the authors tell us what we need to do:

> ". . . Now we go out to our fellows and repair the damage done in the past. We attempt to sweep away the debris which has accumulated out of our effort to live on self-will and run the show ourselves. If we haven't the will to do this, we ask until it comes. . . ."
>
> (pg. 76, para. 3, lines 6-11)

Then, on page 77 the "Big Book" authors provide us with an example of a "Direct Amends." They ask us to let our actions,

Fourth Step Inventory

Assets and Liabilities Checklist from the "Big Book"
pg. 64:1(1-7); pg. 64:3(1-9); pg. 68:1(1-3); pg. 69:1(1-6:edited)

Liabilities Watch for—					**Assets** Strive for—
Resentment	*Ex*	*Myself*	*Court*	*God*	Forgiveness
Fear	*Court*	*Relapse*	*Health*		Faith
Selfishness	*Ex*	*Employer*	(*Friend #1*)		Unselfishness
Dishonesty	(*Ex*)	*Myself*	(*Employer*)	(*Friend #2*)	Honesty
False Pride	*God*	*Employer*			Humility
Jealousy	(*Family Member*)				Trust
Envy					Contentment
Laziness	(*Ex*)	*Employer*	(*Myself*)		Action
Shame	*Friend #2*				*Self-respect*

Example of Assets and Liabilities Checklist with Eight Step Amends List

rather than our words, demonstrate that we have changed. Starting with the fourth line, they write:

> ". . . It is seldom wise to approach (individuals), who still smart from our injustice to (them), and announce that we have gone religious. In the prize ring, this would be called leading with the chin. Why lay ourselves open to being branded fanatics or religious bores? We may kill a future opportunity to carry a beneficial message. But (they are) sure to be impressed with a sincere desire to set right the wrong. (They are) going to be more interested in a demonstration of good will than in our talk of spiritual discoveries."
>
> (pg. 77, lines 4-14, edited)

One of the most difficult amends to make is to someone we genuinely don't like. But, whether we like the person or not, we must proceed. On page 77, starting with the ninth line in the first paragraph, we find:

> ". . . Nevertheless, with (those) we dislike, we take the bit in our teeth. It is harder to go to an enemy than to a friend, but we find it much more beneficial to us. We go to (them) in a helpful and forgiving spirit, confessing our former ill feeling and expressing our regret."
>
> (pg. 77, para. 1, lines 9-14, edited)

The authors make it clear what we are to do about our debts, which is to pay them. We may not like the sacrifice required to make good on our bills, but sacrifice we must. The process forces us to rely on God for the strength and courage to make good on **"past misdeeds."** Under God's direction, we find it much easier to make restitution than we ever thought possible. In the second paragraph on page 78, they state:

> "Most (of us) owe money. We do not dodge our creditors. Telling them what we are trying to do, we make no bones about our (past); they usually know (of our difficulties) anyway, whether we think so or not. . . .
> . . . Approached in this way, the most ruthless creditor will sometimes surprise us. Arranging the best deal we can we let these people know we are sorry. Our (problem) has made us slow to pay. We must lose our fear of creditors no matter how far we have to go, for we are liable to (relapse) if we are afraid to face them."
>
> (pg. 78, para. 2, lines 1-4, 6-12, edited)

Keep in mind that courage is not the absence of fear. Courage is facing the fear and walking through it.

The authors suggest we ask others for help before we make some of our more difficult amends. We need direction, preferably from someone who understands the inventory and amends process. In the second paragraph on page 79 and the first paragraph on page 80, they caution us not to create further harm as we clean up our side of the street:

> "Usually, however, other people are involved. Therefore, we are not to be the hasty and foolish martyr who would needlessly sacrifice others to save (themselves). . .

> "Before taking drastic action which might implicate other people we secure their consent. If we have obtained permission, have consulted with others, asked God to help and the drastic step is indicated we must not shrink."
>
> (pg. 79, para. 2, lines 1-3 and pg. 80, para. 1, lines 1-5, edited)

In the first paragraph on page 83, we learn how to make a "Living Amends:"

> "Yes, there is a long period of reconstruction ahead. We must take the lead. A remorseful mumbling that we are sorry won't fill the bill at all. . . . So we clean house . . . asking each morning in meditation that our Creator show us the way of patience, tolerance, kindliness and love."
>
> (pg. 83, para. 1, lines 1-3, 7-10, edited)

The "Living Amends" is straightforward. We live, to the best of our ability, as a recovered member of the Twelve-Step community.

This is one of the greatest amends we can make to our family and friends. As the "Big Book" authors write, **"Our behavior will convince them more than our words."**

The "Amends-in-Kind" is described in the first paragraph on page 82:

> ". . . Good generalship may decide that the problem be attacked on the

Fourth Step Inventory

Assets and Liabilities Checklist from the "Big Book"
pg. 64:1(1-7); pg. 64:3(1-9); pg. 68:1(1-3); pg. 69:1(1-6:edited)

Liabilities Watch for—					**Assets** Strive for—
Resentment	*Ex*	*Myself*	*Court*	*God*	Forgiveness
Fear	*Court*	*Relapse*	*Health*		Faith
Selfishness	*Ex*	*Employer*	(*Friend #1*) → Direct		Unselfishness
Dishonesty	(*Ex*) → Living	*Myself*	(*Employer*) → Living	(*Friend #2*) → Direct	Honesty
False Pride	*God*	*Employer*			Humility
Jealousy	(*Family Member*) → Letter				Trust
Envy					Contentment
Laziness	(*Ex*) → In-Kind	*Employer*	(*Myself*) → Living		Action
Shame	*Friend #2*				*Self-respect*

Example of Assets and Liabilities Checklist with Ninth Step Type of Amends Added

> flank rather than risk . . . face-to-face combat."
>
> (pg. 82, para. 1, lines 8-10, edited)

An "Amends-in-Kind" implies doing something "instead of" or "in place of." For example, if you and your partner decide that a "Direct Amends" would only make a situation worse, you can develop an alternative plan of action, such as taking a Beginners' Meeting into a halfway house or prison, volunteering at a homeless shelter or assisted living facility, or making a service commitment to a Twelve-Step group.

In the third paragraph on page 83, the "Big Book" authors give us directions on what to do if we can't make amends to someone face-to-face:

> "There may be some wrongs we can never fully right. We don't worry about them if we can honestly say to ourselves that we would right them if we could. Some people cannot be seen—we send them an honest letter."
>
> (pg. 83, para. 3, lines 1-5)

Pertaining to amends, Step Nine states, "**except when to do so would injure them or others.**" In the first paragraph on page 80, the authors write, "**Before taking drastic action which might implicate other people we secure their consent.**" Unsolicited letters can cause more harm than good, not only for the recipient but also for those he or she is presently involved with. The key to letter writing is to "let it go and move on."

In the early days, many amends letters were sent without a name, an address, a return name, or a return address on the envelope. Of significance is that these letters went exactly where they needed to go in order for the sender to heal.

Today we see a variation on this theme. After the letter is written and read aloud to the sharing partner, it is burned. The outcome is the same. The letter goes where it needs to go for us to recover, without hurting anyone in the process.

So, together the sharing partners decide the type of amends to be made. They role-play the possible outcomes until it becomes clear which type of amends is most appropriate under the circumstances. Again, the types of amends are: "Direct Amends," "Living Amends," "Amends-in-Kind," and "Amends to Those Who Cannot be Seen."

Dr. Bob, one of our Twelve-step pioneers, learned that he could not recover until he made his amends. He accomplished this in one day. On page 156, starting with the first paragraph, we read about Dr. Bob's Ninth Step:

> "One morning he took the bull by the horns and set out to tell those he feared what his trouble had been. He found himself surprisingly well received, and learned that many knew of his (problem). Stepping into his car, he made the rounds of people he had hurt. He trembled as he went about, for this might mean ruin, particularly to a person in his line of business.
>
> "At midnight he came home exhausted, but very happy. He has not (relapsed) since. . . ."
>
> (pg. 156, para. 1, lines 1-8; para. 2, lines 1-2, edited)

This concludes our presentation of Step Nine. If you are not sure how to make a specific amends, please ask your sharing partner for help. Together, you can work out the details on how to proceed.

During the next session, we will take Steps Ten, Eleven and Twelve. But, before we end this session, we would like to lay the groundwork for the Eleventh Step. This is the Step that puts us in direct contact with the **"Power greater than ourselves"** that will solve our problems.

Step Eleven reads:

"Sought through prayer and meditation to improve our conscious contact with God as we understood (God), praying only for knowledge of (God's) will for us and the power to carry that out."

Many refer to **"prayer and meditation"** as two-way prayer. When we pray, we do the talking, and when we meditate, we do the listening. We listen in order to receive guidance directly from the One **"who has all knowledge and power."** This is what a conscious contact is all about–a **"personal relationship"** with the **"Spirit of the Universe."**

The "Big Book" authors have been preparing us for this conscious contact by interspersing references about two-way prayer throughout the book. So, before we actually take Step Eleven next session, we are going to take time now to look at some of the "Big Book" passages that pertain to guidance.

Let's start by defining the word, "guidance." The dictionary explains that "to guide" means "to lead, direct, influence, or regulate." Two synonyms are "to disclose" and "to show."

When we look in the "Big Book" for passages that refer to guidance, we find there are at least twenty-six of them. If something is mentioned at least twenty-six times, it must be important. Earlier this session, we read one of the passages, which is within the first paragraph on page 83:

> ". . . So we clean house . . . asking each morning in meditation that our Creator **SHOW** us the way of patience, tolerance, kindliness and love."
>
> (pg. 83, para. 1, lines 7-10, edited)

In this passage, the "Big Book" authors instruct us to conduct a daily "quiet time." It is during this period of meditation that God will **SHOW** us, in other words, God will guide us, to a new way of living based on **PATIENCE, TOLERANCE, KINDLINESS** and **LOVE.**

There are many more references to guidance, starting all the way back at the First Step. We're only going to mention a few of them.

On page 13 of the "Big Book," Bill W., one of the Twelve-Step pioneers, writes about **"prayer and meditation."** Starting with the third line in the fourth paragraph, he states:

> ". . . I was to sit quietly when in doubt, asking only for **DIRECTION** and strength to meet my

problems as (God) would have me. . . ."
(pg. 13, para. 4, lines 3-5, edited)

When we ask God for **DIRECTION** and strength, we are calling upon the **"Spirit of the Universe"** to guide us **"in a way which is indeed miraculous."**

It is essential that we **"sit quietly,"** especially during periods of stress or uncertainty, so we can clearly hear what God has to say. Meditation is based on the belief that a **"Power greater than ourselves"** speaks to those who are willing to listen. We write down the thoughts and ideas we receive so we can separate the guidance that comes from **"infinite God rather than our finite selves."**

How do we determine the source of the messages we receive? We use the test we described last session, which is the test for self-will vs. God's will. The "Big Book" authors show us how to use this test three times. In the Fourth Step we apply the test in connection with our assets and liabilities checklist to decide if we need to make amends. We also use this test in our Tenth and Eleventh Steps.

Let's look again at how the authors use the test for self-will vs. God's will in the Fourth Step:

Test for self-will	Test for God's will
Resentment	**Forgiveness**
Fear	**Faith**
Selfishness	**Unselfishness**
Dishonesty	**Honesty**

We use this same test to examine what we put on paper during our "quiet time." If what we have written is based in forgiveness, faith, unselfishness **AND** honesty, we can consider this guidance to be of spirit. If what we have written consists of resentment, fear, selfishness **OR** dishonesty, we can assume this guidance is from self.

On page 57, starting with the third line in the second paragraph, the "Big Book" authors state that the **"Realm of Spirit" "is constantly being revealed"** to us:

> ". . . (God) has come to all who have honestly sought (a spiritual solution to their difficulties).
>
> "When we drew near . . . (God) **DISCLOSED** (the answers) to us!"
>
> (pg. 57, para. 2, lines 3-4; para. 3, lines 1-2, edited)

When we seek God's guidance, we find a **"new power, peace, happiness and sense of direction."** On page 69, starting with the sixth line in the third paragraph, we learn that God will answer our questions, if we just ask:

> ". . . In meditation, we ask God what we should do about each specific matter. The right answer will come, if we want it."
>
> (pg. 69, para. 3, lines 6-8)

In the second paragraph on page 70, we read about some of the things we ask for:

> " . . . We earnestly pray for the right ideal, for **GUIDANCE** in each questionable situation, for sanity, and for the strength to do the right thing. . . ."
>
> (pg. 70, para. 2, lines 1-4)

These are just a few examples from the "Big Book" on **"prayer and meditation."** Hopefully, they are sufficient to get started with Step Eleven.

In the next session, the "Big Book" authors will provide us with guidelines on what to do **"on awakening," "when we retire,"** and **"through the day."** Here are a few things to keep in mind, **"on awakening."**

Each morning we practice a "quiet time," similar to the way Bill W. described his "quiet time" on page 13 of the "Big Book." During this time alone with God, we discover the most important and practical thing we can ever learn–how to listen to the "God-consciousness within." All we need is the willingness to try it honestly. Every person who has done this consistently and sincerely has found that it really works.

1. Set aside time to meditate.

At first, we may have difficulty getting quiet and listening. But with practice, we will find the "quiet time" more and more effective and productive, because the "quiet time" brings us closer and closer to the Indwelling Spirit. The "quiet time" is an essential part of our morning surrender, because when we surrender our will, we can then listen for God's will.

God has a plan for our lives and during our "quiet times" much of this plan is revealed to us. The quality of the guidance we receive is in direct proportion to the amount of time we spend alone with God.

2. Relax and take it easy.

We can enhance our spiritual connection by practicing some deep breathing exercises. There are many techniques available. They help put the mind at rest, shut down the "committee," and alleviate obsessions and cravings.

We assume a comfortable position and enter into our "quiet time" with an expectancy that it will work. We maintain an attitude of reverence, gratitude and humility.

We let our imagination "go loose." Thoughts, ideas and impressions will begin to come into our heart and mind. We need to be alert and receptive to all of them.

3. Write down or dictate, either during or after the period of meditation, the guidance you receive, so you won't forget it and have something to review "at night."

Writing or otherwise recording our thoughts, feelings and images is the key to the process. We don't try to clear our mind. Rather, we just monitor it.

We don't sort out or edit what we receive until our "quiet time" is over. A thought, feeling or image comes quickly and it can escape just as quickly if we do not record it.

Be honest. Record everything.

4. Test the guidance to determine if it is based in "the realm of the material"(self-will) or "the Realm of Spirit" (God's will).

We take a good look at what we have recorded. Not every thought, feeling or image we receive comes from God.

How do we distinguish between those that come from self-will and those that are of God's will? We test them using the first four items on the Fourth Step Assets and Liabilities Checklist. As we mentioned earlier, the liabilities are the OR side of the sheet and the assets are the AND side.

5. Check the guidance with a sharing partner or partners.

When the flow of thoughts, feelings and images slows down, we stop. We take a good look at what we have written, and we discuss our guidance with a sharing partner or partners. Since we can only see ourselves through others, we need to check our guidance with those who are also actively engaged in two-way prayer. We talk over what we have written because, "More light comes in through two windows then one."

6. Follow through with the guidance that passes the test of forgiveness, faith, unselfishness and honesty.

We carry out the guidance that appears to us and others to be "God's will," but, we cannot be completely sure of the guidance until we go through with it. "A rudder will not guide a boat until the boat is moving." Very often the results will convince us we are on the right track. Keep in mind that God will never guide us to do anything that is not based in forgiveness, faith, unselfishness AND honesty.

Some people don't feel comfortable meditating and writing at the same time. If this is the case, we can use our fingertips to record our guidance. This is how it works:

> As soon as a thought, feeling or image comes into our mind, we touch our thumb to our first finger to capture the essence of it.
>
> When another thought, feeling or image comes, we capture it by touching our thumb to our second finger.
>
> We keep capturing our thoughts, feelings and images until the end of our meditation period.
>
> We again touch our thumb to our finger or fingers in order to recall what we have captured.
>
> We then write down or relay the messages that were on our fingertips.

Remember, our Creator has given us free will. We are free not to listen to the God directed messages we receive. But, we must be prepared to accept the consequences if we choose not to follow God's plan for our lives.

By living in **"the sunlight of the Spirit,"** we are given the **"strength, inspiration and direction"** to change lives, starting with our own. Miracles are about to occur, and we look forward to hearing about them next session.

Are there any questions?

Chapter 4

Session #4–Steps 10, 11 and 12

WELCOME to session number four of ***Back to the Basics of Recovery***. This is the payoff–the reward for our efforts, which is to overcome our **"seemingly hopeless state of mind and body."**

We have demystified the Twelve Steps and shown you just how simple this program truly is. However, we must keep in mind that recovery is an ongoing process. We don't just take the Steps once and then **"rest on our laurels."** We must repeat the process again and again in order to **"keep in fit spiritual condition."** By taking the Steps over and over, we enlarge and expand upon the **"spiritual awakening"** that brings about **"a new freedom and a new happiness."**

Our names are ____________ and ____________, and we will be your guides for this meeting. During this session we will take Steps Ten, Eleven and Twelve.

The Tenth Step is a summary of Steps Four through Nine. The Eleventh Step shows us how to enhance our spiritual connection with the **"One who has all power"** through prayer and meditation. The Twelfth Step provides us with guidelines for carrying our life-saving message to others. Let's start with the Tenth Step. It reads:

Continued to take personal inventory and when we were wrong promptly admitted it.

In Steps One, Two and Three, we made the decisions that put us on the spiritual path. In Steps Four through Nine, we took the actions necessary to remove those things that had been blocking us from the **"God-consciousness within."** Now, we're ready to grow into the promised spiritual awakening that will enable us to **"be of maximum service to God and the people about us."**

The key to the Tenth Step is the word **"continue."** In the second paragraph on page 84, the "Big Book" authors emphasize the importance of continuing to take the Steps:

> "This . . . brings us to *Step Ten*, which suggests we continue to take personal inventory and continue to set right any new mistakes as we go along. We vigorously commenced this way of living as we cleaned up the past. We have entered the world of the Spirit. Our next function is to grow in understanding and effectiveness. This is not an overnight matter. It should continue for our lifetime. . . ."
>
> (pg. 84, para. 2, lines 1-8, edited)

In this paragraph, the authors explain how to live, one day at a time. We call this our twenty-four hour plan. We continue to take inventory, continue to make amends, continue to forgive, and continue to help others every day.

Please note that starting with this paragraph on page 84, the "Big Book" authors dramatically change the tone of the book. Until this point, they have used the words, **"next," "at once," "promptly,"** and **"we waste no time"** to emphasize that we take the first nine Steps quickly. Now, at Step Ten, they tell us that,

"This is not an overnight matter. It should continue for our lifetime." Here, they suggest we take Steps Ten, Eleven, and Twelve on a daily basis for the rest of our lives.

On page 84, starting with the eighth line in the second paragraph, the authors summarize Steps Four through Nine. Once again, they are emphatic that we take these Steps quickly:

> ". . . Continue to watch for selfishness, dishonesty, resentment, and fear. When these crop up, we ask God at once to remove them. We discuss them with someone immediately and make amends quickly if we have harmed anyone. Then we resolutely turn our thoughts to someone we can help. Love and tolerance of others is our code."
>
> (pg. 84, para. 2, lines 8-14)

Let's look at the first three sentences in this passage in more detail. **"Continue to watch for selfishness, dishonesty, resentment, and fear."** (These are the first four liabilities from our Fourth Step inventory.) **"When these crop up, we ask God at once to remove them."** (This sentence summarizes Steps Six and Seven.) "We discuss them with someone immediately" (This is Step Five.) **"and make amends quickly if we have harmed anyone."** (This refers to Steps Eight and Nine.)

Again, when the authors ask us to make this daily review, they basically use the same words they used when they introduced us to the inventory and amends process earlier in the book. Here, they write, **"at once," "immediately,"** and **"quickly."**

Also in this paragraph, the "Big Book" authors present the test for "self-will vs. God's will" for a second time. In the second session, we described how we use this test to check the liabilities side of our Fourth Step inventory to determine if we need to make amends. In the Tenth Step, the authors advise us to apply this same test, with minor variations, to our daily inventory. Here, they instruct us **"to watch for selfishness, dishonesty, resentment and fear."**

The authors even provide us with specific directions on how to rid ourselves of these self-centered behaviors. First, we must realize they are not consistent with God's plan for our lives. Next, we take the actions necessary to move from self-will to God's will. We discuss our shortcomings with our sharing partner, ask the **"One who has all power"** to remove them, and, if necessary, **"set right the wrong(s)."** We then try to help someone else.

The "Big Book" authors state that if we routinely follow this process, God will remove our addictive and compulsive behaviors. This is another of the many promises we find throughout the text of the book. In the third paragraph on page 84, they write:

> "And we have ceased fighting anything or anyone. . . . For by this time sanity will have returned. We will seldom be interested in (our old way of living). If tempted, we recoil from it as from a hot flame. We react sanely and normally and we will find that this has happened automatically. We will see that our new attitude . . . has been given us without any thought or effort on our part. It just comes! That is the

> miracle of it. We are not fighting it, neither are we avoiding temptation. We feel as though we had been placed in a position of neutrality—safe and protected. We have not even sworn off. Instead, the problem has been removed. It does not exist for us. . . . That is how we react so long as we keep in fit spiritual condition."
>
> (pg. 84, para. 3, lines 1-4; pg. 85, lines 1-9, 11-12, edited)

How do we **"keep in fit spiritual condition?"** By taking a daily inventory. What is our reward? A daily reprieve.

Now it is time to take Step Ten. The directions are in the second paragraph on page 84.

We would like everyone who is ready to take the Tenth Step to answer this question in unison. It is:

"Will you continue to take personal inventory and continue to set right any new mistakes as you go along?"

And, your answer is?

(Have the participants answer the Tenth Step question.)

Thank you. According to the "Big Book" authors, those who answered "yes" to this question have taken Step Ten.

Now, let's move on to the Eleventh Step. It reads:

Sought through prayer and meditation to improve our conscious contact with God as we understood (God), praying only for knowledge of (God's) will for us and the power to carry that out.

This is the Step we prepared for last session. We are now going to examine **"prayer and meditation"** in more detail. Then, we will practice the Eleventh Step by taking a five minute "quiet time" in order to listen to and record our guidance from the indwelling spirit.

The description of Step Eleven is found on pages 85 through 88 of the "Big Book." In the third paragraph on page 85, the authors ask us to conduct an Eleventh Step on a regular basis:

> "*Step Eleven* suggests prayer and meditation. We shouldn't be shy on this matter of prayer. Better men (and women) than we are using it constantly. It works, if we have the proper attitude and work at it. . . ."
>
> (pg. 85, para. 3, lines 1-2; pg. 86, lines 1-2, edited)

"Prayer and meditation" puts us in direct contact with the **"Power greater than (ourselves) which will solve (our) problem."** Starting with the second line on page 86, they provide us with some of the details:

> ". . . It would be easy to be vague about this matter. Yet, we believe we can make some definite and valuable suggestions."
>
> (pg. 86, lines 2-4)

Then the authors provide step-by-step instructions of how to practice two-way prayer. They tell us what we are to do at night, in the morning, and throughout the day.

At night, we review the day's activities. In the first paragraph on page 86, the authors write:

> "When we retire at night, we constructively review our day. Were we resentful, selfish, dishonest or afraid? Do we owe an apology? Have we kept something to ourselves which should be discussed with another person at once? Were we kind and loving toward all? What could we have done better? Were we thinking of ourselves most of the time? Or were we thinking of what we could do for others, of what we could pack into the stream of life?"
>
> (pg. 86, para. 1, lines 1-9)

This paragraph contains the third reference to the test for "self-will vs. God's will." The "Big Book" authors once again have made minor changes to the test they presented to us in the Fourth and Tenth Steps. Nevertheless, it is still the opposite of the test for God's will based on the assets side of our Fourth Step inventory sheet:

Test for self-will	Test for God's will
Resentful	**Forgiving**
Selfish	**Unselfish**
Dishonest	**Honest**
Afraid	**Faithful**

We can also use this same test during our morning meditation to check our guidance.

In the second paragraph on page 86, the authors provide us with directions for conducting a daily "quiet time":

> "On awakening let us think about the twenty-four hours ahead. We consider our plans for the day. Before we begin, we ask God to direct our thinking, especially asking that it be divorced from self-pity, dishonest or self-seeking motives."
>
> (pg. 86, para. 2, lines 1-5)

Let's look at the third sentence again. It reads, "**Before we begin, we ask God to direct our thinking . . .**" Please concentrate on these words. They are very important. "**Before we begin,**"—before we begin what? Before we begin listening to God. How do we know that we're supposed to listen to God? Because, right afterward, it says, **"we ask God to direct our thinking."** If we ask God to direct our thinking, doesn't it stand to reason that some of our next thoughts or feelings just might be of a spiritual nature? What do we do with these thoughts and feelings? We write them down. Why? So we won't forget them.

After we write down our thoughts and feelings, we test them to determine the source. We do this because not everything we receive is from the Indwelling Spirit. Some of the messages may be our ego at work. However, with time and practice we will begin to trust **"our vital sixth sense"** and be able to separate the spiritual from the **"ego-centric."** Starting with the first sentence on page 87, the "Big Book" authors explain:

> "What used to be the hunch or the occasional inspira-

> tion gradually becomes a working part of the mind. Being still inexperienced and having just made conscious contact with God, it is not probable that we are going to be inspired at all times. We might pay for this presumption in all sorts of absurd actions and ideas. Nevertheless, we find that our thinking will, as time passes, be more and more on the plane of inspiration. We come to rely upon it."
>
> (pg. 87, lines 1-9)

Again, please note the change in the tempo of the book. Here the authors write, **"gradually"** and **"as time passes."** They are emphasizing that this part of the program is going to take practice–practice–practice.

The authors are emphatic that all of our questions will be answered. In the third paragraph on page 86, they reveal how the **"God consciousness within"** is going to reply to our requests for help:

> "In thinking about our day we may face indecision. We may not be able to determine which course to take. Here we ask God for inspiration, an intuitive thought or a decision. We relax and take it easy. We don't struggle. We are often surprised how the right answers come after we have tried this for a while. . . ."
>
> (pg. 86, para. 3, lines 1-6)

According to the "Big Book" authors, God is going to communicate with us through **"inspiration, an intuitive thought, or a decision."** If the **"One who has all power"** is going to provide us with **"the right answers,"** wouldn't it be a good idea to record them so we don't forget them?

We end our **"prayer and meditation"** by asking God to guide us during our daily activities. In the first paragraph on page 87, the "Big Book" authors write:

> "We usually conclude the period of meditation with a prayer that we be shown all through the day what our next step is to be, that we be given whatever we need to take care of such problems. We ask especially for freedom from self-will, and are careful to make no request for ourselves only. . . ."
>
> (pg. 87, para. 1, lines 1-6)

The "Big Book" authors then describe what to do anytime we become troubled or confused. We relax and ask for guidance. Starting with the third paragraph on page 87, the authors tell us:

> "As we go through the day we pause, when agitated or doubtful, and ask for the right thought or action. We constantly remind ourselves we are no longer running the show, humbly saying to ourselves many times each day 'Thy will be done.' We are then in much less danger of excitement, fear, anger, worry, self-pity, or foolish decisions. We become much more efficient. We do not tire so easily, for we are not burning up energy foolishly as we did when we were trying to arrange life to suit ourselves.
>
> "It works—it really does."
>
> (pg. 87, para. 3, lines 1-3; pg. 88, lines 1-7; para.1, line 1)

This is an ironclad guarantee. **"It works!"** From first-hand experience, we can state that two-way prayer has been working in our lives ever since we began a daily "quiet time."

But, what if we don't receive any God given thoughts, images or feelings? Let us assure you, this can happen at any time. Remember, all **"we really have is a daily reprieve contingent upon the maintenance of our spiritual condition."** If we don't feel **"the Presence of God,"** it means we have work to do. Maybe we've taken back our will in some area of our lives, or, maybe we haven't made a necessary amends. If this is the case, we take the actions that reconnect us to the **"One who has all power."**

Starting with the second paragraph on page 88, the "Big Book" authors state, once again, that we need God's help:

> "We . . . are undisciplined. So we let God discipline us in the simple way we have just outlined.
>
> "But this is not all. There is action and more action. 'Faith without works is dead. . . .' "
>
> (pg. 88, para. 2, lines 1-2; para. 3, lines 1-2, edited)

In order for two-way prayer to be effective, we must continually practice being in the presence of God. If we do the work, we will receive the rewards: a life filled with **"power, peace, happiness, and a sense of direction."**

We are now going to take a five minute "quiet time" so each of us can make contact with the **"Spirit of the Universe"** and receive divine guidance right now. Please write down or capture on your fingertips any thoughts, images or feelings you receive during this period of silence.

[Five minutes of silence]

Thank you. As we mentioned last session, guidance can consist of thoughts, images, sounds or feelings. We realize these messages can be very personal and are normally discussed with only your sharing partner. However, if you believe the group will benefit from what you have received, we ask that you consider sharing it with us now. In addition, you will be helping those who are still struggling with the Eleventh Step to see how **"God constantly disclose(s) more to you and to us."**

Who's willing to share what they have written or captured on their fingertips?

[For the next 10 minutes, have the participants share their guidance.]

Thank you. Whether you shared guidance or listened to others share their guidance, you have taken Step Eleven. Now, we can proceed to the Twelfth Step. It reads:

Having had a spiritual awakening as the result of these steps, we tried to carry this message to (others), and to practice these principles in all our affairs.

Now that we've made conscious contact with the **"Spirit of the Universe,"** we have received the greatest gift of this program—a spiritual awakening. God is now guiding us **"in a way which is indeed miraculous."**

Chapter 7, in its entirety, is devoted to carrying our message of recovery to others. In the first paragraph on page 89, the "Big Book" authors tell us how we expand upon our new God-consciousness:

> PRACTICAL EXPERIENCE shows that nothing will so much insure immunity from (relapse) as intensive work with other(s). It works when other activities fail. This is our *twelfth suggestion:* Carry this message to other(s) . . . ! You can help when no one else can. You can secure their confidence when others fail. . . ."
>
> (pg. 89, para. 1, lines 1-7, edited)

When **WE** work with others, **OUR** lives change. In the second paragraph on page 89, the authors state:

> "Life will take on new meaning. To watch people recover, to see them help others, to watch loneliness vanish, to see a fellowship grow up about you, to have a host of friends—this is an experience you must not miss. We know you will not want to miss it. Frequent contact with newcomers and with each other is the bright spot of our lives."
>
> (pg. 89, para. 2, lines 1-7)

On pages 89 through 103, the "Big Book" authors provide us with specific instructions on how to carry our lifesaving message of recovery to others. They offer many valuable suggestions on these pages.

In the first paragraph on page 100, the "Big Book" authors

inform us that we grow spiritually when we work with newcomers:

> "Both you and (your sharing partner) must walk day by day in the path of spiritual progress. If you persist, remarkable things will happen. When we look back, we realize that the things which came to us when we put ourselves in God's hands were better than anything we could have planned. Follow the dictates of a Higher Power and you will presently live in a new and wonderful world, no matter what your present circumstances!"
>
> (pg. 100, para. 1, lines 1-9, edited)

Back on page 63, the authors stated that God is our **"new Employer."** Now, in the second paragraph on page 102, the "Big Book" authors provide us with a new job description:

> "Your job now is to be at the place where you may be of maximum helpfulness to others, so never hesitate to go anywhere if you can be helpful. You should not hesitate to visit the most sordid spot on earth on such an errand. Keep on the firing line of life with these motives and God will keep you unharmed."
>
> (pg. 102, para. 2, lines 1-6)

This concludes our presentation of Step Twelve as found in our "Big Book." Let God guide you when you make your Twelfth Step calls and the **"Spirit of the Universe"** will keep you safe and protected. In addition, by relying upon guidance you **WILL "be of maximum service to God and the people about (you)."**

Being of service to others is critical to our continued growth and the maintenance of our sobriety. Keep in mind that one of the primary services we can perform is to take prospective members through the Twelve Steps. Each time we do this, we learn more about our lifesaving program and gain additional insight into the **"All Powerful Creator"** who is at the heart of our new way of living.

Now, all that's left is to practice the principles of the Twelve Steps in all our affairs. If we do this, we will remain in the **"sunlight of the Spirit"** for the rest of our lives.

We are now ready to take the Twelfth Step. We would like everyone who is ready to take this Step to answer this question in unison. This is the Twelfth Step question.

"Will you carry this message to others?"

And, your answer is?

(Have the participants answer the Twelfth Step question.)

Thank you. According to the "Big Book" authors, those who answered "yes" to this question have taken Step Twelve.

We are going to close this session by reading the second, third and fourth paragraphs on page 164. Here the "Big Book" authors make yet one more statement concerning the importance of guidance and the necessity of working with others:

> "Our book is meant to be suggestive only. We realize we know only a little. God will constantly disclose

more to you and to us. Ask (God) in your morning meditation what you can do each day for the (person) who is still sick. The answers will come, if your own house is in order. But obviously you cannot transmit something you haven't got. See to it that your relationship with (God) is right, and great events will come to pass for you and countless others. This is the Great Fact for us.

"Abandon yourself to God as you understand God. Admit your faults to (God) and to your fellows. Clear away the wreckage of your past. Give freely of what you find and join us. We shall be with you in the Fellowship of the Spirit, and you will surely meet some of us as you (travel) the Road of Happy Destiny.

"May God bless you and keep you—until then."

(pg. 164, para. 2, lines 1-10; para. 3, lines 1-6; para. 4, line 1, edited)

Please, don't let anyone talk you out of your miracle. We have taken the Twelve Steps the way Bill W., Dr. Bob, and many of the pioneers intended for them to be taken. As the "Big Book" authors write in the second paragraph on page 132:

" . . .We have recovered, and have been given the power to help others."

(pg. 132, para. 2, lines 5-6)

We welcome all who have taken the Twelve Steps to the **"fourth dimension of existence."** We thank you for the opportunity to be your guides for this miraculous spiritual journey.

Are there any questions?

[After all questions have been answered, the meeting leader brings the session to a close.]

(Optional)

Please remain seated. We will close this meeting with a moment of silence followed by:

the Serenity Prayer, or
the Third Step Prayer, or
the Seventh Step Prayer, or
any other agreed upon Prayer.

Appendices

Appendices

Handouts for the Four Sessions of *Back to the Basics of Recovery*

Summary of the Handouts for the Four Sessions

Suggested Guidelines for the Sharing Partner

Suggested "Big Book" Passages for Taking the Twelve Steps (Two-sided)

Four Spiritual Activities Illustrated (Two-sided)

Taking Steps Four through Nine using an Assets and Liabilities Checklist (Two-sided)

Fourth Step Inventory (Blank)

Fourth Step Questions

Fourth Step Inventory (After Answering Questions)

Explanation of Terms: Assets and Liabilities Checklist

Fourth Step Inventory (With Eighth Step Amends List)

Fourth Step Inventory (With Types of Ninth Step Amends Added)

The "Voice of Addiction" vs. the "Voice of Recovery"

Four Paths of Divine Guidance

Handouts for the Four Sessions of *Back to the Basics of Recovery*
(Continued)

Listening to the God-consciousness Within (Two-sided)

Eleventh Step Guidance Meeting Format (Two-sided)

The Twelve Steps of Recovery Modified for all Addictive and Compulsive Behaviors

Back to the Basics of Recovery Modified Format

"It works–it really does."

Handouts for the Four Sessions

Stapled Packet: Eighteen Handouts From One-Sided to Two-Sided (Nine Pages Total)

1	Summary of Handouts for the Four Sessions
2	Suggested Guidelines for the Sharing Partner
3-4	Suggested "Big Book" Passages for Taking the Twelve Steps
5-6	Four Spiritual Activities Illustrated with the Square and Triangle
7-8	Taking Steps Four through Nine using an Assets and Liabilities Checklist
9	Fourth Step Inventory (Blank)
10	Fourth Step Questions
11	Fourth Step Inventory (After Answering Questions)
12	Explanation of Terms–Assets and Liabilities Checklist
13	Fourth Step Inventory (With Eighth Step Amends List)
14	Fourth Step Inventory (With Types of Ninth Step Amends Added)
15	The "Voice of Addiction" vs. the "Voice of Recovery"
16	Four Paths of Divine Guidance
17-18	Listening to the "God-consciousness Within" (Two-Sided)

Unstapled: Four Handouts from One-Sided to Two-Sided (Two Pages Total)

19	Fourth Step Inventory (Blank)
20	Fourth Step Questions
21-22	Eleventh Step Guidance Meeting Format (Two-Sided)

Back to The Basics of Recovery
Suggested Guidelines

For the Sharing Partner:

A. Your primary obligation is to attend all four sessions in order to take the Twelve Steps and offer encouragement and moral support to your partner. The conditions for being a sharing partner are:

1. to be actively involved in your own Twelve-Step recovery,
2. to be willing to listen to what your partner has to say, and
3. to keep everything that is shared strictly confidential.

B. We will guide you through the Twelve Steps by reading the appropriate parts of the "Big Book" to you. If you follow the directions provided by the "Big Book" authors, you too will experience the **"personality change sufficient to bring about recovery."**

C. The Fourth Step consists of a simple assets and liabilities checklist that you fill out during the second session. If you believe your partner satisfies the conditions of a **"closemouthed, understanding friend,"** please discuss your checklist with him or her. If your inventory contains specific items that you feel must be shared with a third party such as a person of the clergy, an attorney, a psychologist, or a counselor, explain this to your sharing partner. Make a commitment to your partner as to when, where, and with whom you will share those portions of your checklist.

D. Between the third and fourth sessions, share your Eleventh Step guidance with your partner so he or she can see how two-way prayer is working in your life.

Back to the Basics of Recovery

Suggested "Big Book" Passages for Taking the Twelve Steps (Fourth Edition ~ Standard Size "Big Book")

Introduction

Who are we? pg. xiii: 5 (1) and pg. xiv: 0 (1-6)
What do we have to offer? pg. 17: 3 (1-6)

Surrender (Steps 1, 2 and 3)

Step 1: ***We admitted we (had a problem)—that our lives had become unmanageable.***

Physical symptoms: pg. xxx: 5 (1-3, 5-8); pg. 44: 1 (4-7)
Mental symptoms: pg. xxviii: 4 (1-6) and pg. xxix: 0 (1-9); pg. 23: 1 (3-10) and pg. 23: 2 (1-9); pg. 30: 1 (4-10)
Psychic change: pg. xxix: 1 (1-7)
Unmanageability: pg. 52: 2 (3-8)
First Step question: pg. 30: 2 (1-3)

Step 2: ***Came to believe that a Power greater than ourselves could restore us to sanity.***

Lack of Power: pg. 45: 1 (1-4) and pg. 45: 2 (1-3)
Where do we find the Power? pg. 55: 2 (1-7), pg. 55: 3 (5-7)
Look within: pg. 55: 4 (3-4)
What if the newcomer doesn't believe? pg. 46: 1 (3-8)
Second Step question: pg. 47: 2 (1-3)

Step 3: ***Made a decision to turn our will and our lives over to the care of God as we understood (God).***

A life run on self-will: pg. 60: 4 (1-8)
Selfishness blocks us from God's will: pg. 62: 1 (1-8) and pg. 62: 2 (1-8)
A life guided by the vision of God's will: pg. 62: 3 (1-4, 6-8) and pg. 63: 1 (1-4)
Third Step prayer: pg. 63: 2 (2-8)

Sharing (Steps 4, 5, 6 and 7)

Step 4: ***Made a searching and fearless moral inventory of ourselves.***

Explanation: pg. 63: 4 (1-2) and pg. 64: 0 (1-5)
Assets and liabilities checklist: pg. 64: 1 (1-7)
Fill out liabilities side of the checklist first: pg. 64: 2 (1-6)
Sponsor does the writing: pg. 13: 3 (1-4)
What do we inventory?
Resentments: pg. 64: 3 (1-2, 6-9)
  We overcome our resentments with forgiveness: pg. 66: 4 (1-2), pg. 67: 0 (1-8), and pg. 67: 1 (1-2)
Fears: pg. 68: 1 (1-3)
  We overcome our fears with faith: pg. 68: 2 (1-4) and pg. 68: 3 (4-10)
Harms: pg. 69: 1 (1-6)
  We overcome our harms with amends: pg. 69: 3 (2-4)

Step 5: ***Admitted to God, to ourselves, and to another human being the exact nature of our wrongs.***

We share our inventory: pg. 72: 2 (4-10)

With whom? pg. 73: 4 (1), pg. 74: 0 (1-9), and pg. 74: 1 (1-4)
This Step may be temporarily postponed: pg. 74: 2 (2-6)
How do we take this Step: pg. 75: 1 (1-4)

Step 6: *Were entirely ready to have God remove all these defects of character.*

Explanation: pg. 76: 1 (1-7)
Sixth Step question: pg. 76: 1 (3-5)

Step 7: *Humbly asked (God) to remove our shortcomings.*

Seventh Step prayer: pg. 76: 2 (1-7)

Amends (Steps 8 and 9)

Step 8: *Made a list of all persons we had harmed, and became willing to make amends to them all.*

Explanation: pg. 76: 3 (2-5)

Step 9: *Made direct amends to such people wherever possible, except when to do so would injure them or others.*

Explanation: pg. 76: 3 (6-11)
Specific amends:
- Direct: To people we dislike: pg. 77: 1 (9-14)
- Direct: To creditors: pg. 78: 2 (1-12)
- Living: Patience, tolerance, kindliness and love: pg. 83: 1 (1-3, 7-10)
- In-kind: pg. 82:1 (8-10)
- Letters: To people who cannot be seen: pg. 83: 3 (1-5)

Guidance (Steps 10, 11 and 12)

Step 10: *Continued to take personal inventory and when we were wrong promptly admitted it.*

Explanation: pg. 84: 2 (1-8)
Tenth Step process: pg. 84: 2 (8-14)
Tenth Step question: pg. 84: 2 (2-3)

Step 11: *Sought through prayer and meditation to improve our conscious contact with God <u>as we understood (God)</u>, praying only for knowledge of (God's) will for us and the power to carry that out.*

Explanation of two-way prayer: pg. 85: 3 (1-2) and pg. 86: 0 (1-4)
When we retire: pg. 86: 1 (1-9)
Upon awakening: pg. 86: 2 (1-5)
How does God communicate with us? pg. 86: 3 (1-6)
How did God communicate with Bill W.? pg. 14: 2 (1-8)
Practice, practice, practice: pg. 87: 0 (1-9)
Throughout the day: pg. 87: 3 (1-3), pg. 88: 0 (1-7), and pg. 88: 1 (1)

Step 12: *Having had a spiritual awakening as the result of these steps, we tried to carry this message to (others), and to practice these principles in all our affairs.*

Explanation: pg. 89: 1 (1-7) and pg. 89: 2 (1-7)
Twelfth Step question: pg. 89: 1 (5)

Close

Program summary: pg. 164: 2 (1-10), pg. 164: 3 (1-6), and pg. 164: 4 (1)
There is a solution: pg. 25: 1 (1-12) and pg. 25: 2 (1-9)

The Four Spiritual Activities
from which the Twelve Steps evolved

One: Surrender (Steps 1, 2 and 3)

Surrender is a three-part process that produces a change in perception. In Step One, we admit we have a problem. In Step Two, we either believe or become willing to believe that a **"Power greater than ourselves"** will solve our problem. In Step Three, we make a commitment to turn our problem over to **"this Power"**–a power that resides inside each and every one of us.

It is our selfish, self-centeredness that cuts us off from the Power. When it's all about me-me-me-me-me, we are in what we call the "prison cell of addiction." In terms of our spiritual journey, we are at Step Zero.

During our surrender, we ask the Power to free us from this prison cell–from **"the bondage of self."** When we do this, we see the world differently. Instead of feeling isolated and alone, we begin to feel connected to the Power and to **"our fellows."**

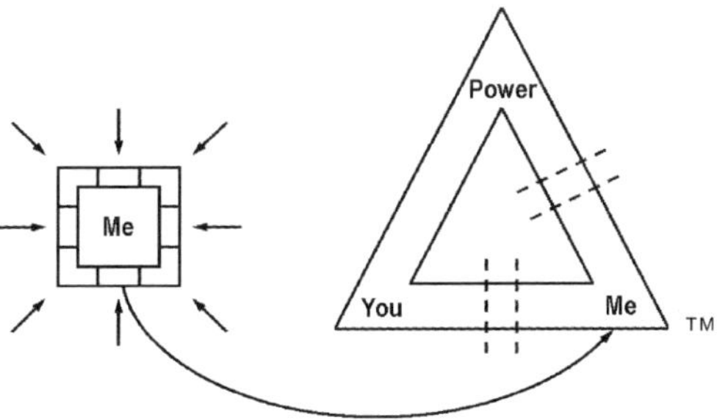

Two: Sharing (Steps 4, 5, 6 and 7)

Sharing involves identifying the manifestations of self that have kept us blocked from the **"Power greater than ourselves"** and from our families, friends, acquaintances and associates. In Step Four, we identify our shortcomings by making an inventory of our "grosser handicaps"

In Step Five, we discuss these shortcomings with a sharing partner. In Steps Six and Seven, we turn our assets as well as our liabilities over to the **"One who has all power"** and ask that we be given back what we need in order **"to be of maximum service to God and the people about us."**

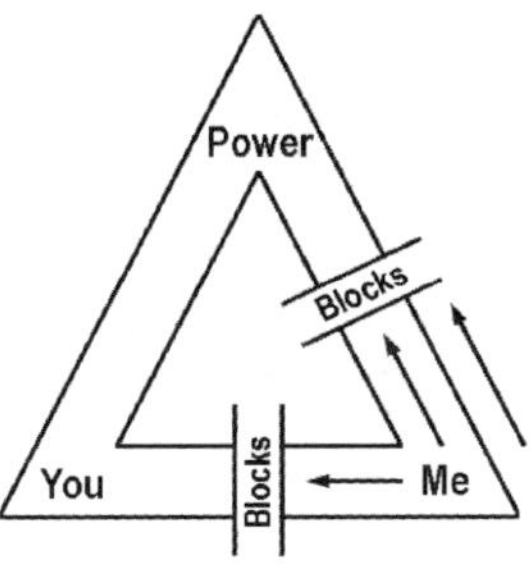

Three: Amends (Steps 8 and 9)

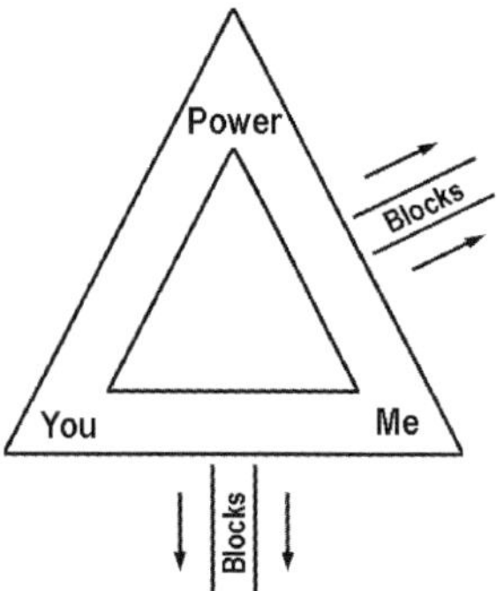

In Steps Eight and Nine, **"We go out to our fellows and repair the damage done in the past."** When we make amends to those we have harmed and forgive those who have harmed us, the **"All Powerful, Guiding, Creative Intelligence"** removes the blocks that have separated us from the God of our understanding and from our fellows.

We let our actions rather than our words demonstrate to those we have harmed that we have changed. We are now acting according to God's will rather than according to self-will.

Four: Guidance (Steps 10, 11 and 12)

When we practice Steps Ten, Eleven and Twelve on a daily basis, we remain connected to the "Power" and to each other. This is the essence of recovery.

In Step Ten we make a commitment to practice Steps Four through Nine on a regular basis. We do this so we can keep the channels open between "You," "Me" and the "Power."

We practice Step Eleven daily. We conduct a morning "quiet time" in order to receive Divine guidance. We check what we receive against the Four Standards of Honesty, Purity, Unselfishness and Love, and we discuss our guidance with our sharing partner or partners.

Throughout the day, **"we pause when agitated or doubtful"** and ask for guidance. **"We relax and take it easy. We don't struggle."** We **"ask for the right thought or action."** and **"that we be shown all through the day what our next step is to be."**

In the evening, we review our guidance to make sure we have carried out what we have been directed to do. We ask ourselves, **"Were we kind and loving toward all?"** and, **"Were we thinking of what we could do for others?"**

In Step Twelve, we rely upon Divine guidance when carrying our life-saving message of recovery to others. We let the Power radiate through us to them.

In addition, we can receive Divine guidance by way of others. We call this three-way prayer–the Power communicating to us through another person. We also can petition the Power to intercede directly in other people's lives, and they can petition the Power to intercede in ours. The arrows point in all directions. We are now living in **"the sunlight of the Spirit.**

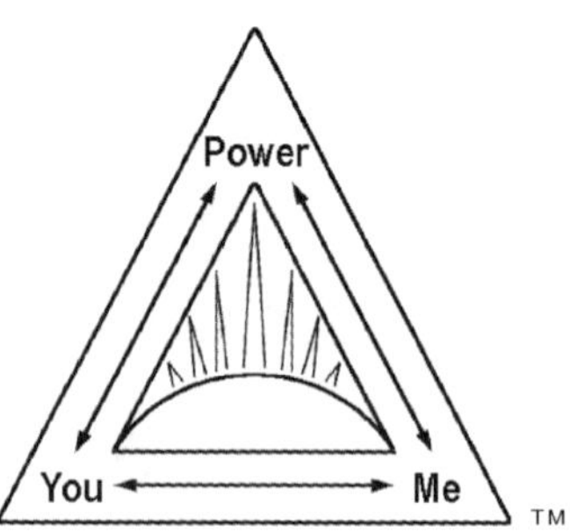

Back to the Basics of Recovery

Taking Steps Four through Nine using an Assets and Liabilities Checklist

Assumptions:

1. The sharing partners have an hour or so to spend together.
2. Each has made a commitment to be a "closed-mouthed, understanding friend."
3. They agree to ask each other questions and fill out each other's checklist.

The inventory consists of the events and situations that are bothering the sharing partner right now. If he or she has completed previous inventories, those items need not to be inventoried again. It usually takes only a few incidents to get down to the "causes and conditions" that are blocking the partner from a more intimate and effective two-way relationship with the "One who has all power."

The inventory is based on the principle that, "The healing is in the sharing, not in the writing." Another principle is, "We put nothing in writing that can incriminate us or others." That's why the inventory consists of nothing more than some names and a few circles.

First, the sharing partners fold their checklists so the assets are hidden from view.

Next, they ask each other the following questions:

Resentment Inventory------ Who or what are you angry at?

Fear Inventory---------------Who or what are you afraid of?

Harms Inventory-------------Toward whom have you been selfish?
Where have you been dishonest?
What about false pride—do you see yourself as better than or less than others?
Are you jealous of any relationship?
Do you envy anyone's possessions?
Where have you been lazy?

To the right of the applicable liabilities, the partner who is asking the questions (the "questioner") writes the generic equivalent of the names that represent the "people, institutions (and) principles" to be inventoried (Step Four). It is far more beneficial to take a few incidents through Step Nine than to write down so many names that the person answering the questions (the "respondent") becomes overwhelmed or discouraged and gives up on the process.

After the names have been added to the checklist, the "questioner" asks the "respondent" to describe the circumstances surrounding each of them. During the course of the discussion, the "questioner" explains to the "respondent" that, "we resolutely look for our own mistakes" and we "disregard the other person entirely" (Step Five).

If the "respondent" is angry about an event or situation, the "questioner" lets him or her know that we overcome our resentments with forgiveness. If the "respondent" is afraid, the "questioner" explains that we overcome our fears with faith. If the "respondent" has offended or has adversely affected someone, the "questioner" tells him or her that we make good on our past misdeeds with amends.

If the sharing partners agree that an amends needs to be made, the "questioner" circles the appropriate name or names. The circled names become the amends list (Step Eight).

Then, the "questioner" unfolds the checklist so they can look at the assets. Those assets with the least number of names to the left of them are the assets the "respondent" already has. Those assets with the most names to the left of them are the assets that will be strengthened as the result of making amends.

The "questioner" asks the "respondent" if he or she wants the liabilities removed. If the "respondent" does, then the "questioner" asks, "Are you now ready to let God remove from you all the things which you have admitted are objectionable?" (Step Six). If the "respondent" still wishes to hold on to any of the liabilities, they pray together for the willingness for those shortcomings to be removed.

Then, they say a prayer together (Step Seven).

> **"My Creator I am now willing that you should have all of me, good and bad. I pray that you now remove from me every single defect of character which stands in the way of my usefulness to you and my fellows. Grant me strength, as I go out from here, to do your bidding. Amen."**

Next, they talk about the details of each amends. For each event or situation, they decide which type of amends would be appropriate. The four types of amends described in the "Big Book" are "direct," "living," "in kind," and "amends to those who cannot be seen." They role-play each amends until they both agree on a course of action. They also decide when and where they will meet immediately following the amends so they can discuss what happened and determine if any follow-up action needs to be taken (Step Nine).

With this Assets and Liabilities Checklist, the sharing partners have everything they need to take Steps Four through Nine in about an hour.

Fourth Step Inventory

Assets and Liabilities Checklist from the "Big Book"
pg. 64:1(1-7); pg. 64:3(1-9); pg. 68:1(1-3); pg. 69:1(1-6:edited)

Liabilities Watch for—		**Assets** Strive for—
Resentment		Forgiveness
Fear		Faith
Selfishness		Unselfishness
Dishonesty		Honesty
False Pride		Humility
Jealousy		Trust
Envy		Contentment
Laziness		Action

Assets and Liabilities Checklist

Back to the Basics of Recovery

Fourth Step Questions

Resentment Inventory

1. Who or what are you angry at? ____________

Fear Inventory

2. Who or what are you afraid of? ____________

Harms inventory

3. Toward whom have you been selfish? ____________
4. Where have you been dishonest? ____________
5. What about false pride–do you see yourself as better than or less than others? ____________
6. Are you jealous of any relationship? ____________
7. Do you envy anyone's possessions? ____________
8. Where have you been lazy? ____________

During the discussion of each event or situation, ask your partner to "*resolutely look for (your) own mistakes. . . . Though a situation had not been entirely (your) fault, (you are) to disregard the other person entirely. Where were (you) to blame?"* (pg. 67: 2 (2-3, 4-7), edited).

Ask him or her, "Are you prepared to forgive those toward whom you feel resentment?" If not, then *"we ask God to help us be willing."* (pg. 76: 1 (6-7)).

Ask, "Are you ready to overcome your fear with faith?" Together, *"We ask (God) to remove our fear and direct our attention to what (God) would have us be. At once, we commence to outgrow fear."* (pg. 68: 3 (7-10), edited).

In terms of harms, ask your partner, *"What are you "willing (to do) to set these matters straight?"* (pg. 67: 2 (10-11), edited). Keep in mind there are four types of amends: direct, living, in-kind, and letters. Together, decide what would be the most appropriate *"course of action"* for each incident or circumstance.

Conclude the sharing session with a prayer. (pg. 76: 2 (1-7)).

Fourth Step Inventory

Assets and Liabilities Checklist from the "Big Book"
pg. 64:1(1-7); pg. 64:3(1-9); pg. 68:1(1-3); pg. 69:1(1-6:edited)

Liabilities
Watch for—

Resentment	*Ex*	*Myself*	*Court*	*God*
Fear	*Court*	*Relapse*	*Health*	
Selfishness	*Ex*	*Employer*	*Friend #1*	
Dishonesty	*Ex*	*Myself*	*Employer*	*Friend #2*
False Pride	*God*	*Employer*		
Jealousy	*Family Member*			
Envy				
Laziness	*Ex*	*Employer*	*Myself*	
Shame	*Friend #2*			

Example of Assets and Liabilities Checklist After Answering Questions

Explanation of Terms

Fourth Step Assets and Liabilities Checklist

In the late 1930's, Dr. Bob, one of the pioneers of the Twelve-Step movement, developed an Assets and Liabilities Checklist, which he used to take thousands of people through the inventory and restitution process. Since then, various checklists have been used by sharing partners to bring those **"interested in a spiritual way of life"**to a greater understanding of the shortcomings that have prevented them from finding a spiritual solution to their difficulties, a solution that is based upon establishing an intimate, two-way relationship with the **"One who has all power."**

We have defined these shortcomings–the liabilities that have been blocking us from this **"Power"**–in a way that, hopefully, will provide a clearer understanding of their meaning:

RESENTMENT is the consequence of being angry or bitter toward someone for an extended period of time over some real or imagined insult. It is a hostile or indignant attitude in response to an alleged affront or personal injury.

FEAR is being afraid of losing something we have or not getting something we want. It manifests itself in many ways including phobia, terror, panic, anxiety and worry.

SELFISHNESS is concern only for ourselves, our own welfare or pleasure, without regard for, or at the expense of, others.

DISHONESTY involves theft or deception. It includes taking things that don't belong to us, cheating people out of what is rightfully theirs, and lying to or withholding the truth from others.

FALSE PRIDE is either feeling better than or less than someone else. Feelings of superiority include prejudice about race, education or religious beliefs; and sarcasm–putting someone else down to make us feel better about ourselves. Feelings of inferiority include self-pity, which is excessive concern about our own troubles, and low self-esteem–the lack of self-worth or self-respect.

JEALOUSY has to do with people–being suspicious of another's motives or doubting the faithfulness of a friend.

ENVY has to do with things–wanting someone else's possessions.

LAZINESS means lacking the will or the desire to work. Procrastination, which is postponing or delaying an assigned job or task, is a form of laziness.

Fourth Step Inventory

Assets and Liabilities Checklist from the "Big Book"
pg. 64:1(1-7); pg. 64:3(1-9); pg. 68:1(1-3); pg. 69:1(1-6:edited)

Liabilities Watch for—					Assets Strive for—
Resentment	*Ex*	*Myself*	*Court*	*God*	Forgiveness
Fear	*Court*	*Relapse*	*Health*		Faith
Selfishness	*Ex*	*Employer*	*Friend #1*		Unselfishness
Dishonesty	*Ex*	*Myself*	*Employer*	*Friend #2*	Honesty
False Pride	*God*	*Employer*			Humility
Jealousy	*Family Member*				Trust
Envy					Contentment
Laziness	*Ex*	*Employer*	*Myself*		Action
Shame	*Friend #2*				*Self-respect*

Example of Assets and Liabilities Checklist with Eight Step Amends List

Fourth Step Inventory

Assets and Liabilities Checklist from the "Big Book"
pg. 64:1(1-7); pg. 64:3(1-9); pg. 68:1(1-3); pg. 69:1(1-6:edited)

Liabilities Watch for—					Assets Strive for—
Resentment	*Ex*	*Myself*	*Court*	*God*	Forgiveness
Fear	*Court*	*Relapse*	*Health*		Faith
Selfishness	*Ex*	*Employer*	*Friend #1* → Direct		Unselfishness
Dishonesty	*Ex* → Living	*Myself*	*Employer* → Living	*Friend #2* → Direct	Honesty
False Pride	*God*	*Employer*			Humility
Jealousy	*Family Member* → Letter				Trust
Envy					Contentment
Laziness	*Ex* → In-Kind	*Employer*	*Myself* → Living		Action
Shame	*Friend #2*				*Self-respect*

Example of Assets and Liabilities Checklist with Ninth Step Type of Amends Added

The "Voice of Addiction" vs. the "Voice of Recovery"

Using the "Big Book" Fourth, Tenth and Eleventh Step Tests to Distinguish Self-will from God's Will

Addiction / Self-will (OR)		Recovery / God's Will (AND)

Fourth Step Test

Selfish	←→	Unselfish
Dishonest	←→	Honest
Self-seeking	←→	Forgiving
Frightened	←→	Faithful

"Where had we been selfish, dishonest, self-seeking and frightened?" ("Big Book," p. 67, para. 2, lines 3-4)

Tenth Step Test

Selfishness	←→	Unselfishness
Dishonesty	←→	Honesty
Resentment	←→	Forgiveness
Fear	←→	Faith

"Continue to watch for selfishness, dishonesty, resentment, and fear." ("Big Book," p. 84, para. 2, lines 8-9)

Eleventh Step Test

Resentful	←→	Forgiving
Selfish	←→	Unselfish
Dishonest	←→	Honest
Afraid	←→	Faithful

"Were we resentful, selfish, dishonest or afraid?" ("Big Book," p. 86, para. 1, lines 2-3)

Four Paths of Divine Guidance

As described in the second paragraph on page 14 of the "Big Book"

These were revolutionary and drastic proposals, (The proposals Bill is writing about are the Oxford Group Four Steps of Surrender, Sharing, Amends and Guidance.) ***but the moment I fully accepted them, the effect was electric.*** (Bill feels the sensation of electricity.) ***There was a sense of victory, followed by such a peace and serenity as I had never known.*** (Bill feels the additional sensations of victory, peace and serenity.) ***There was utter confidence.*** (Bill is certain his life is changing.) ***I felt lifted up, as though the great clean wind of a mountain top blew through and through.*** (Bill sees himself on top of a mountain and hears the wind.) ***God comes to most men gradually, but (God's) impact on me was sudden and profound.*** (Bill knows he is having a spiritual experience.)

Method of Communication	Path
True Seeing (Visualizing) Perceiving, detecting or experiencing as if by sight. It includes but is not restricted to seeing or forming a mental image such as a daydream, motion picture, photograph, picture, or painting.	**Sight**
True Hearing (Listening) The process, function, or power of receiving auditory stimuli such as sounds, noises or tones. It includes but is not restricted to "the still small voice," words, music, or songs.	**Sound**
True Feeling (Sensing) A generalized bodily consciousness or sensation. It includes but is not restricted to touch, smell, or feelings of warmth or cold. Manifestations include goose bumps, hair standing up on the back of the neck, or a tightening of the chest or stomach.	**Sensation**
True Awareness (Understanding) Knowledge, or intelligence that produces ideas, concepts or observations. It includes but is not restricted to inspiration, intuition, or revelation.	**Knowing**

Listening to the "God-consciousness Within"

Step Eleven ~ Prayer and Meditation

On Awakening ~ "Big Book" pages 86-87

Each morning, we practice a "quiet time," similar to the way Bill W. described his "quiet time" on page 13 of the "Big Book." During this time alone with God, we discover the most important and practical thing we can ever learn–how to listen to the "God-consciousness within." All we need is the willingness to try it honestly. Every person who has done this consistently and sincerely has found that it really works.

1. Set aside time to meditate.

At first, we may have difficulty getting quiet and listening. But with practice, we will find the "quiet time" more and more effective and productive, because the "quiet time" brings us closer and closer to the Indwelling Spirit. The "quiet time" is an essential part of our morning surrender, because when we surrender our will, we can then listen for God's will.

God has a plan for our lives and during our "quiet times" much of this plan is revealed to us. The quality of the guidance we receive is in direct proportion to the amount of time we spend alone with God.

2. Relax and take it easy.

We can enhance our spiritual connection by practicing some deep breathing exercises. There are many techniques available. They help put the mind at rest, shut down the "committee," and alleviate obsessions and cravings.

We assume a comfortable position and enter into our "quiet time" with an expectancy that it will work. We maintain an attitude of reverence, gratitude and humility.

We let our imagination "go loose." Thoughts, ideas and impressions will begin to come into our heart and mind. We need to be alert and receptive to all of them.

3. Write down or dictate, either during or after the period of meditation, the guidance you receive, so you won't forget it and have something to review "at night."

Writing or otherwise recording our thoughts, feelings and images is the key to the process. We don't try to clear our mind. Rather, we just monitor it.

We don't sort out or edit what we receive until our "quiet time" is over. A thought, feeling or image comes quickly and it can escape just as quickly if we fail to record it.

Be honest. Record everything.

4. Test the guidance to determine if it is based in "the realm of the material" (self-will) or "the Realm of Spirit" (God's will).

We take a good look at what we have recorded. Not every thought, feeling or image we receive comes from God.

How do we distinguish between those that come from self-will and those that are of God's will? We test them using the first four items on the Fourth Step Assets and Liabilities Checklist. As we mentioned earlier, the liabilities are the OR side of the sheet and the assets are the AND side.

5. Check the guidance with a sharing partner or partners.

When the flow of thoughts, feelings and images slows down, we stop. We take a good look at what we have written, and we discuss our guidance with a sharing partner or partners. Since we can only see ourselves through others, we need to check our guidance with those who are also actively engaged in two-way prayer. We talk over what we have written because, "More light comes in through two windows then one."

6. Follow through with the guidance that passes the test of forgiveness, faith, unselfishness and honesty.

We carry out the guidance that appears to us and others to be "God's will," but, we cannot be completely sure of the guidance until we go through with it. "A rudder will not guide a boat until the boat is moving." Very often the results will convince us we are on the right track. Keep in mind that God will never guide us to do anything that is not based in forgiveness, faith, unselfishness AND honesty.

Procedure for Listening (Read Before the Meeting)

During this meeting, we will conduct a five minute "quiet time" in order to make "conscious contact" and receive "guidance." Guidance can take the form of images, thoughts, feelings or inspiration.

We write a brief note about what we saw, heard, felt or realized during our "quiet time." We call this "two-way prayer."

We share the guidance we believe passes the "test" of Forgiveness, Faith, Unselfishness and Honesty, and we feel comfortable sharing with other members of the group.

As we hear others read their guidance, we jot down anything that is especially meaningful to us. When we receive guidance through another person or persons, we call this "three-way prayer."

Eleventh Step Guidance Meeting Format

Good (morning/afternoon/evening). My name is ______________ . I would like to welcome everyone to our Eleventh Step Guidance Meeting

Let's open this meeting with a moment of silence followed by the Serenity Prayer.

I have asked ______________ to read the third paragraph on page 86 of the "Big Book."

I have asked ______________ to read today's daily meditation.

We will now sit in silence for five minutes in order to listen to and record our guidance.

(Five minutes of silence)

If anyone needs more time, please raise your hand.

We will now go around the room. I ask that you share only what you have written without embellishment or explanation. This is called "two-way prayer." If you haven't written anything down, please pass.

(Share "two-way prayer")

Did anyone hear something during the sharing session that he or she feels was directed toward them in addition to the person who shared it? If so, please tell the group what you heard. This is called "three-way prayer"—the "Spirit of the Universe" speaking to us through others. If this has happened to you, please raise your hand.

(Share "three-way prayer")

I would like to thank each of you for participating, either by sharing or by listening. I will now read part of the first and second paragraphs on page 87 of the "Big Book."

Please remain seated. We will close this meeting with the Third and Seventh Step Prayers.

Date: ______________

Two-way and Three-way Prayer

Eleventh Step Guidance Meeting Readings

Serenity Prayer

God, grant me the serenity to accept the things I cannot change, courage to change the things I can, and wisdom to know the difference.

The Third Paragraph on Page 86 the "Big Book."

"In thinking about our day we may face indecision. We may not be able to determine which course to take. Here we ask God for inspiration, an intuitive thought or a decision. We relax and take it easy. We are often surprised how the right answers come after we have tried this for a while. What used to be the hunch or the occasional inspiration gradually becomes a working part of the mind. Being still inexperienced and having just made conscious contact with God, it is not probable that we are going to be inspired at all times. We might pay for this presumption in all sorts of absurd actions and ideas. Nevertheless, we find that our thinking will, as time passes, be more and more on the plane of inspiration. We come to rely upon it."

The First and Second Paragraphs on Page 87 of the "Big Book."

"We usually conclude the period of meditation with a prayer that we be shown all through the day what our next step is to be, that we be given whatever we need to take care of such problems. We ask especially for freedom from self-will, and are careful to make no request for ourselves only. . . .

"If circumstances warrant, we ask our . . . friends to join us in morning meditation. If we belong to a religious denomination which requires a definite morning devotion, we attend to that also. If not members of religious bodies, we sometimes select and memorize a few set prayers which emphasize the principles we have been discussing."

Third Step Prayer

"God, I offer myself to Thee—to build with me and to do with me as Thou wilt. Relieve me of the bondage of self, that I may better do Thy will. Take away my difficulties, that victory over them may bear witness to those I would help of Thy Power, Thy Love, and Thy Way of life. May I do Thy will always!"

Seventh Step Prayer

"My Creator, I am now willing that you should have all of me, good and bad. I pray that you now remove from me every single defect of character which stands in the way of my usefulness to you and my fellows. Grant me strength, as I go out from here, to do your bidding. Amen."

Date: ________________

Two-way and Three-way Prayer

THE TWELVE STEPS OF RECOVERY
For All Addictive and Compulsive Behaviors

1. We admitted we had a problem–that our lives had become unmanageable.
2. Came to believe that a Power greater than ourselves could restore us to sanity.
3. Made a decision to turn our will and our lives over to the care of God *as we understood God.*
4. Made a searching and fearless moral inventory of ourselves.
5. Admitted to God, to ourselves, and to another human being the exact nature of our wrongs.
6. Were entirely ready to have God remove all these defects of character.
7. Humbly asked God to remove our shortcomings.
8. Made a list of all persons we had harmed, and became willing to make amends to them all.
9. Made direct amends to such people wherever possible, except when to do so would injure them or others.
10. Continued to take personal inventory and when we were wrong promptly admitted it.
11. Sought through prayer and meditation to improve our conscious contact with God *as we understood God,* praying only for knowledge of God's will for us and the power to carry that out.
12. Having had a spiritual awakening as the result of these steps, we tried to carry this message to others, and to practice these principles in all our affairs.

The Twelve Steps are adapted from the second edition of the book ***Alcoholics Anonymous***, which is in the public domain. Adapting the Twelve Steps does not mean that Alcoholics Anonymous World Services, Inc. has reviewed or approved the content of this publication, nor that AA agrees with the views expressed herein. AA is a program of recovery from alcoholism ***only***–use of the Twelve Steps in connection with programs and activities that are patterned after AA, but that address other problems, does not imply otherwise.

NOTES

NOTES

NOTES

NOTES

NOTES